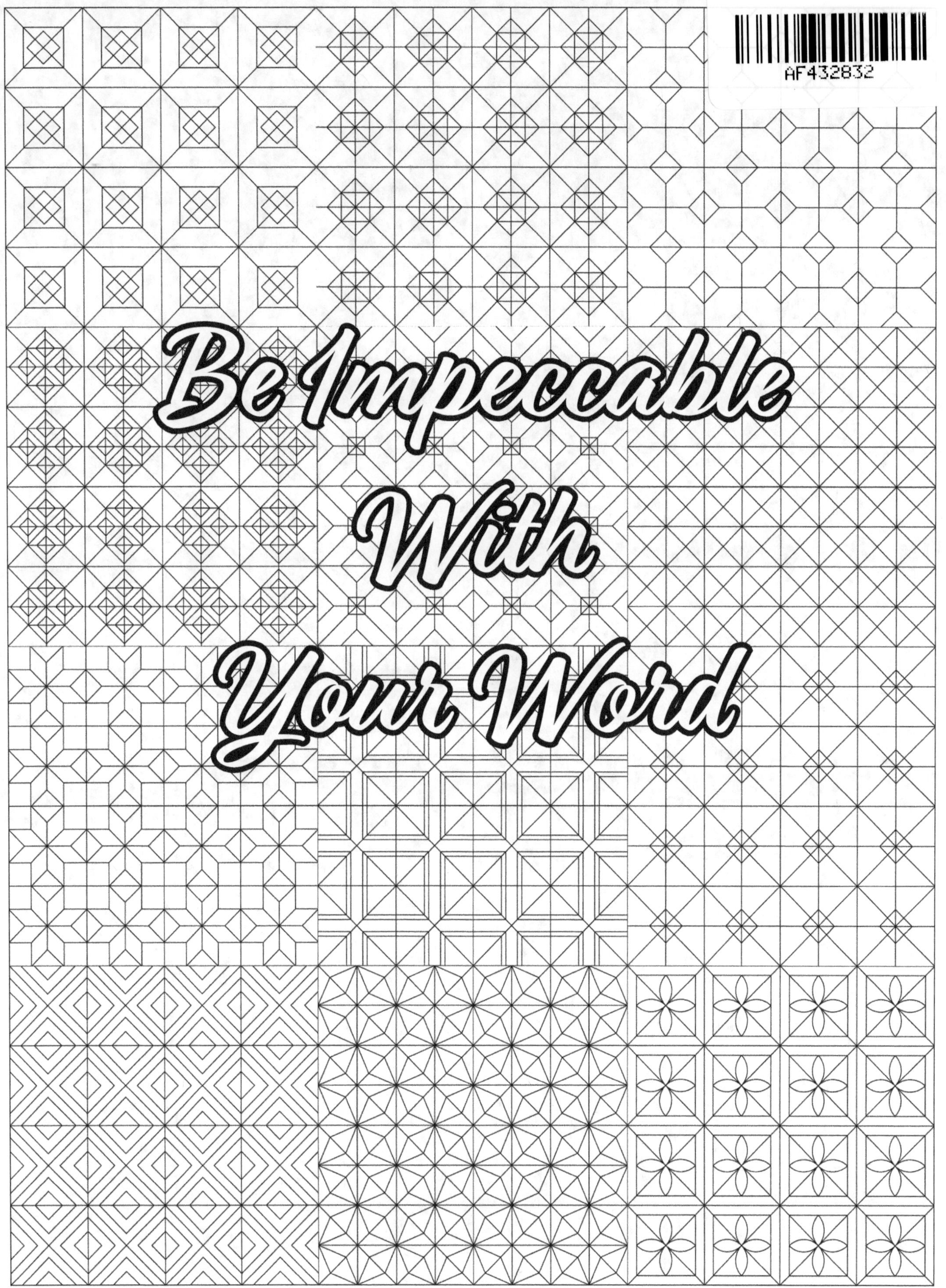

Be Impeccable
With
Your Word

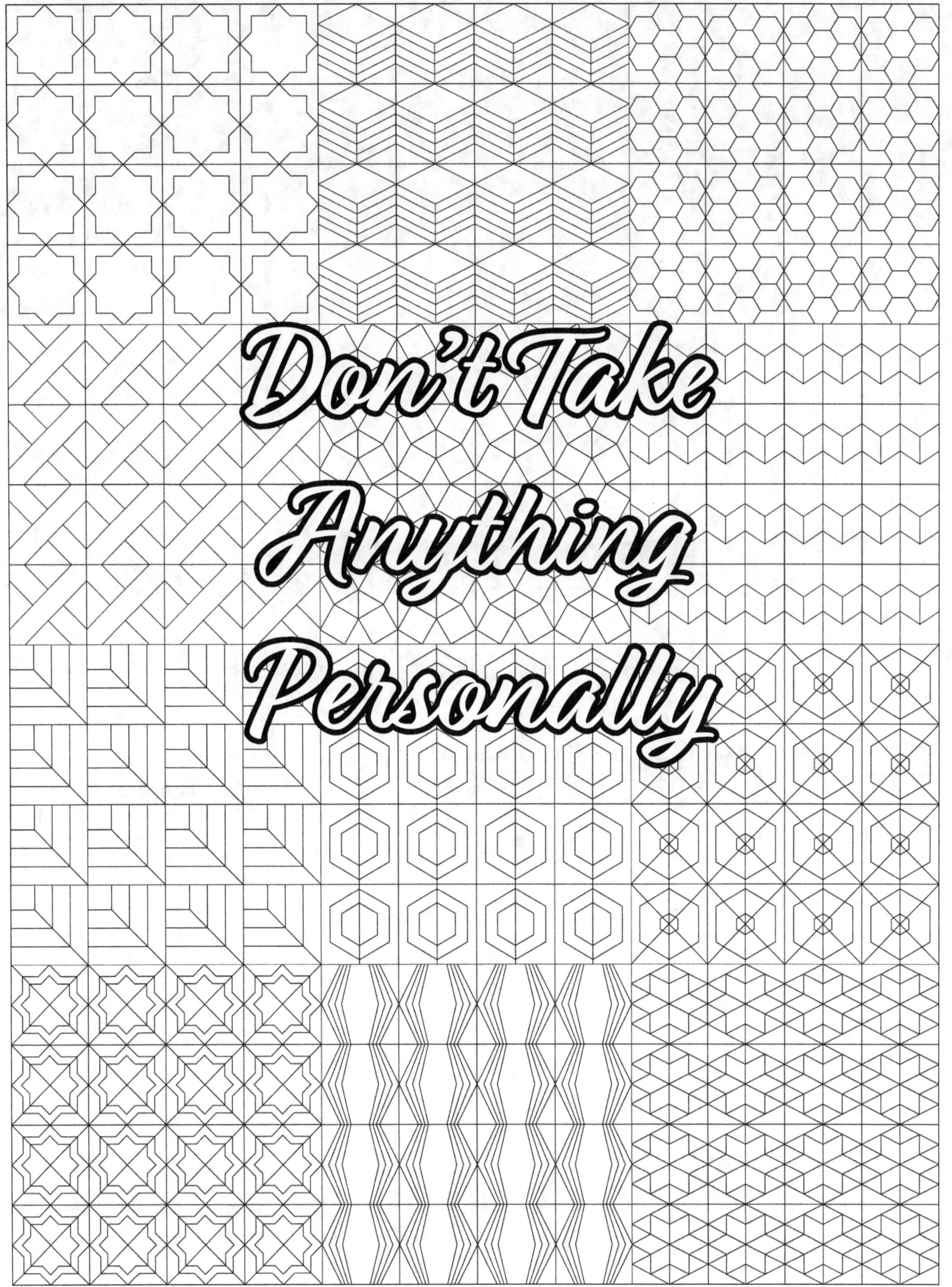

Don't Take
Anything
Personally

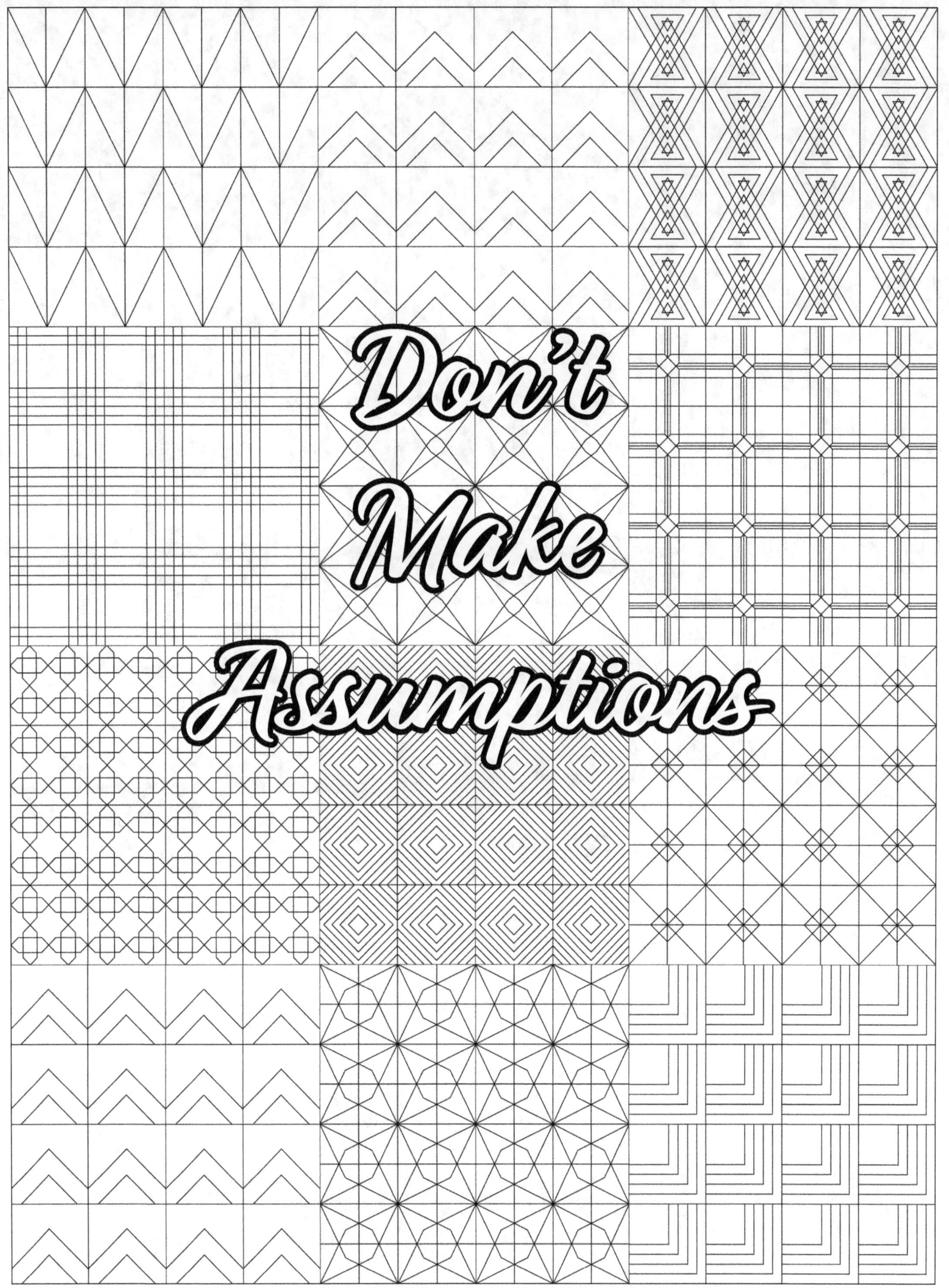

Don't
Make
Assumptions

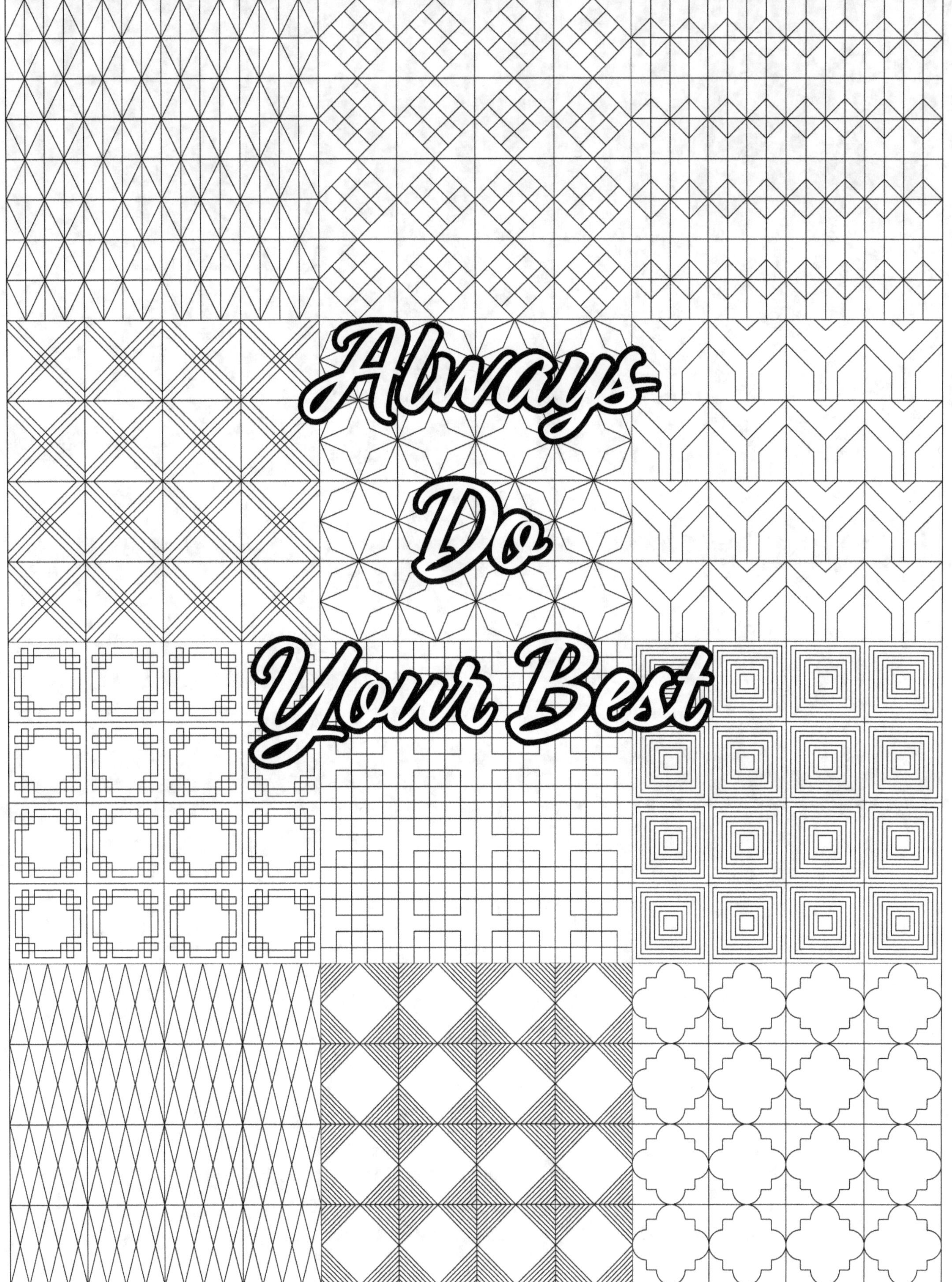
Always
Do
Your Best

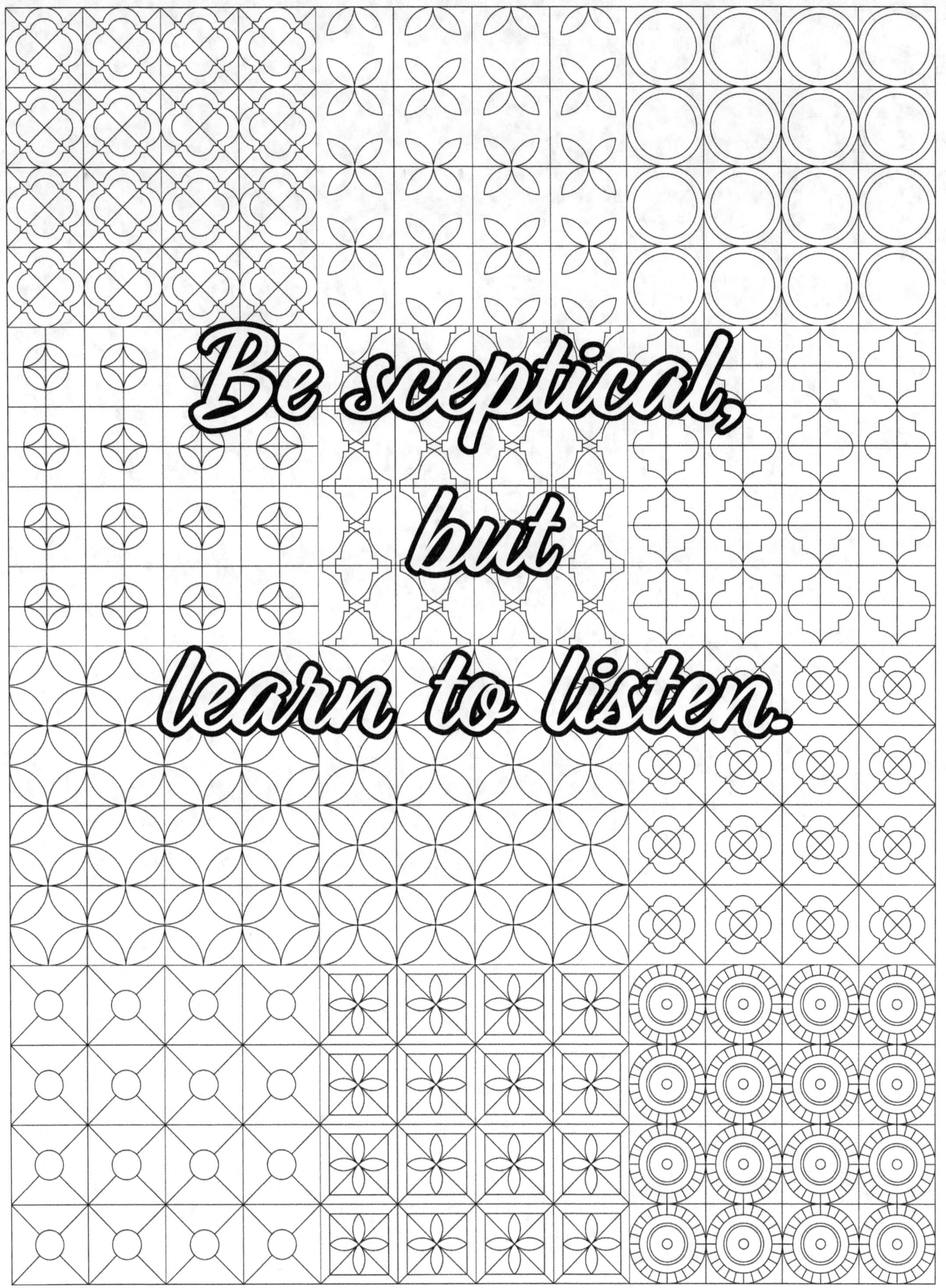
Be sceptical,
but
learn to listen.

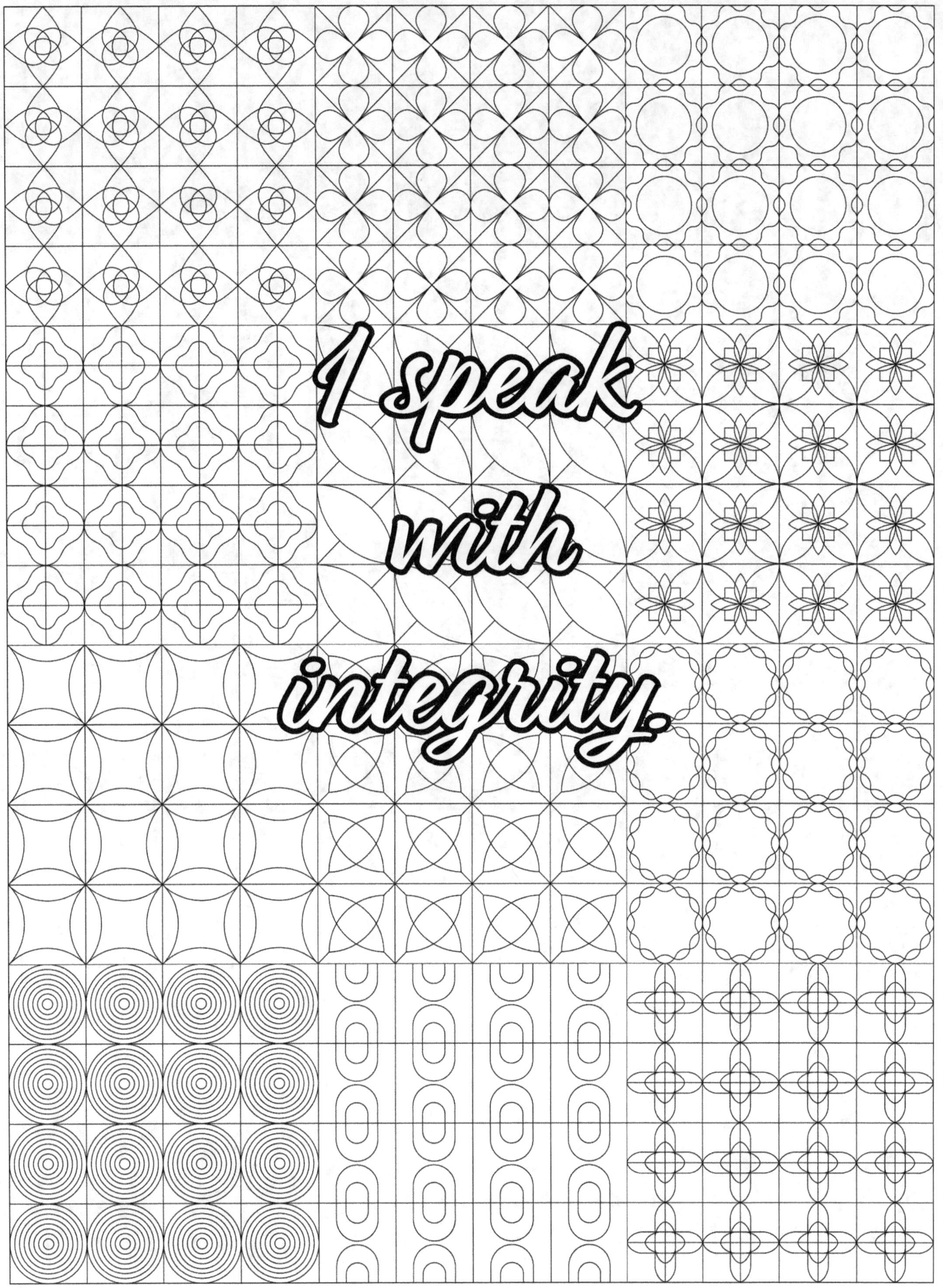
I speak
with
integrity.

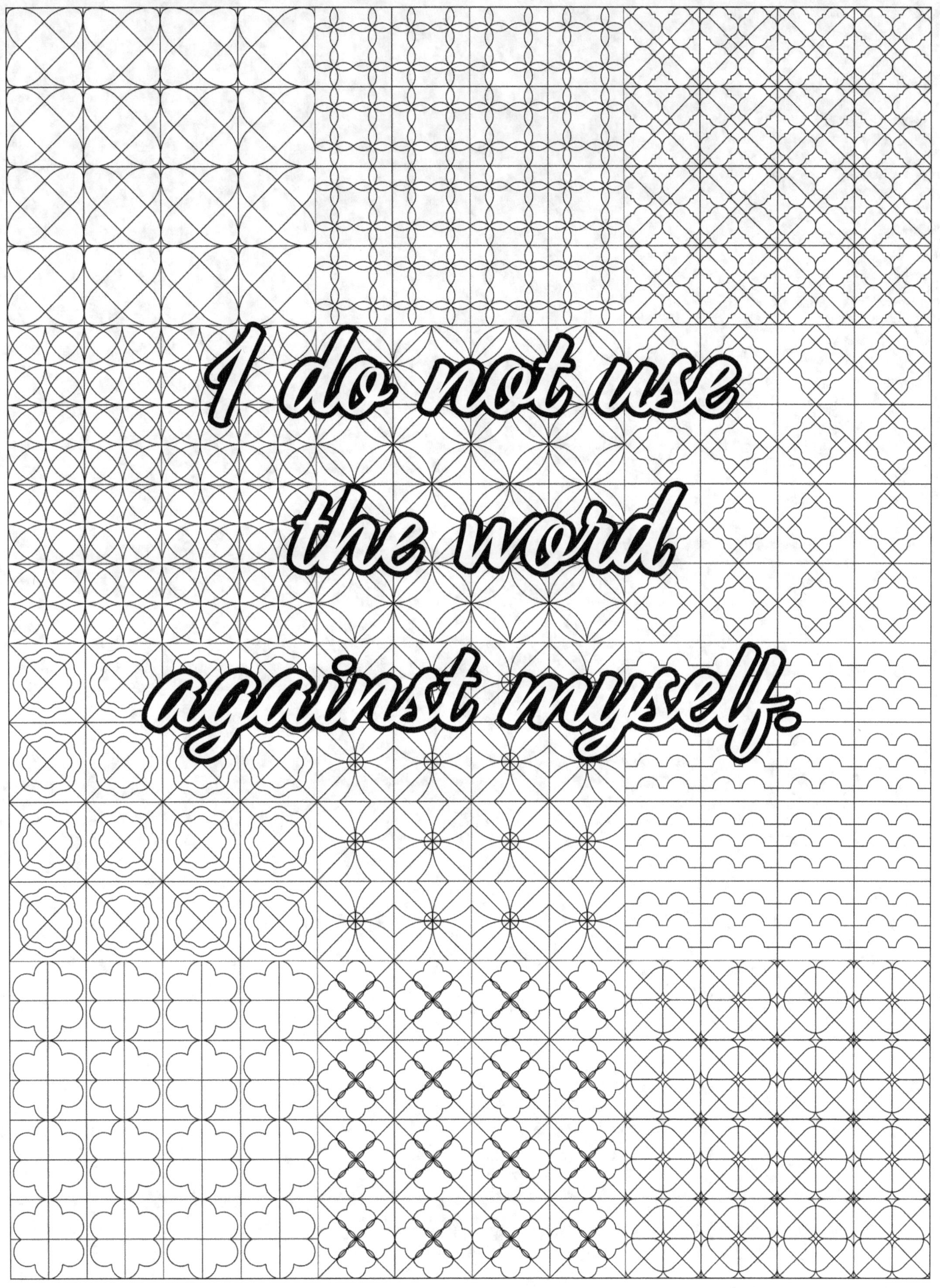

I do not use
the word
against myself.

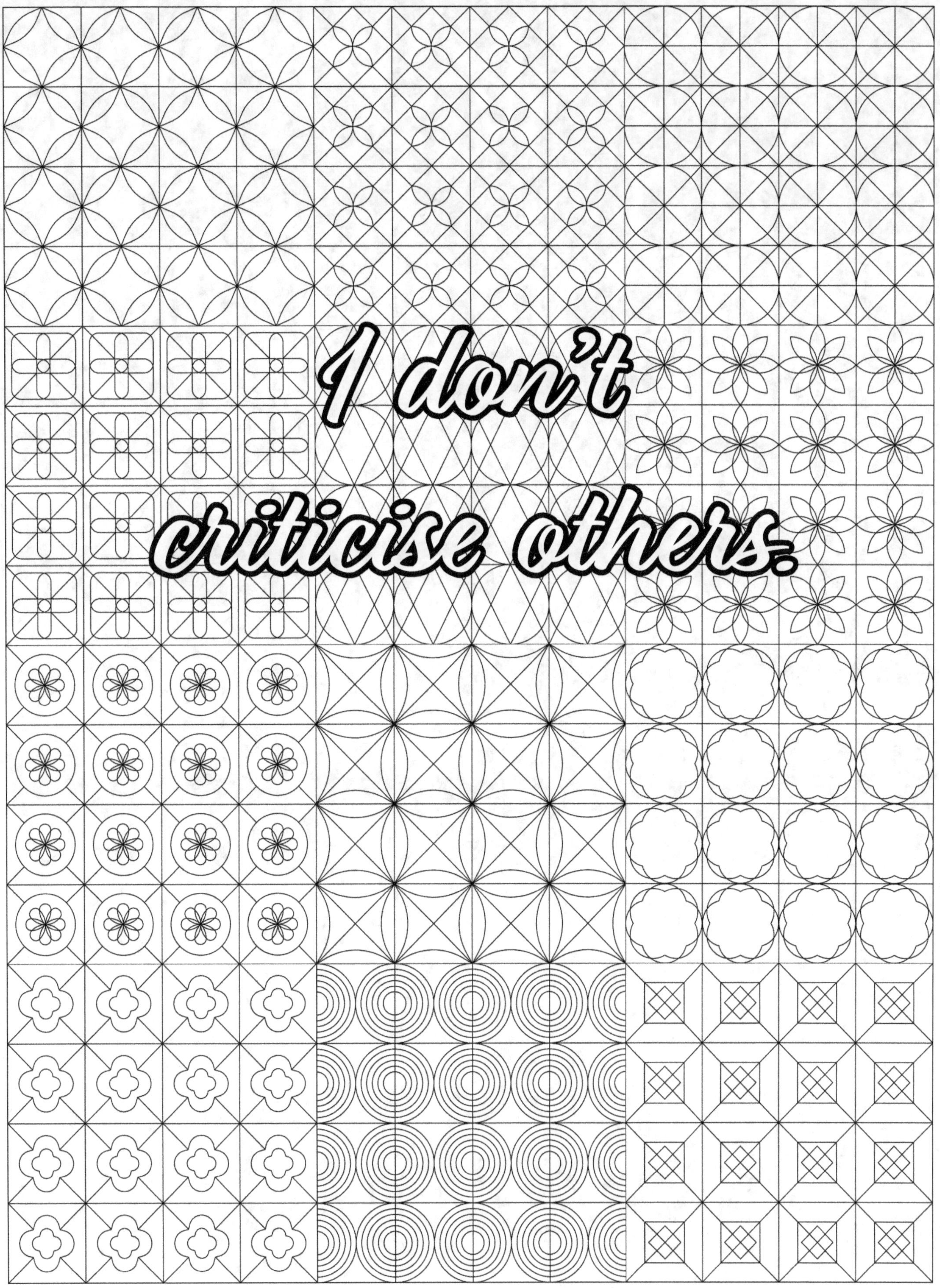
I don't
criticise others.

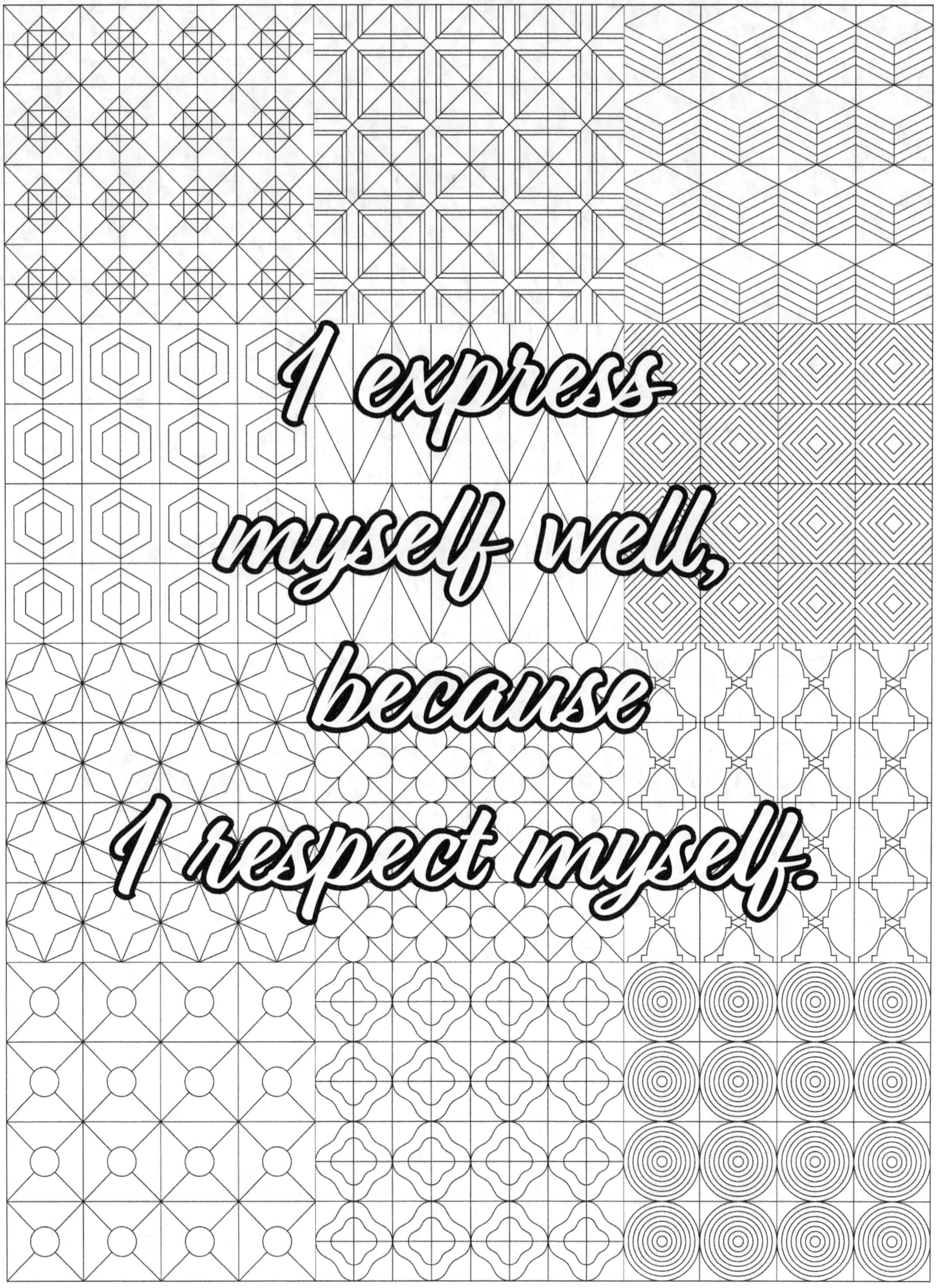

I express myself well, because I respect myself.

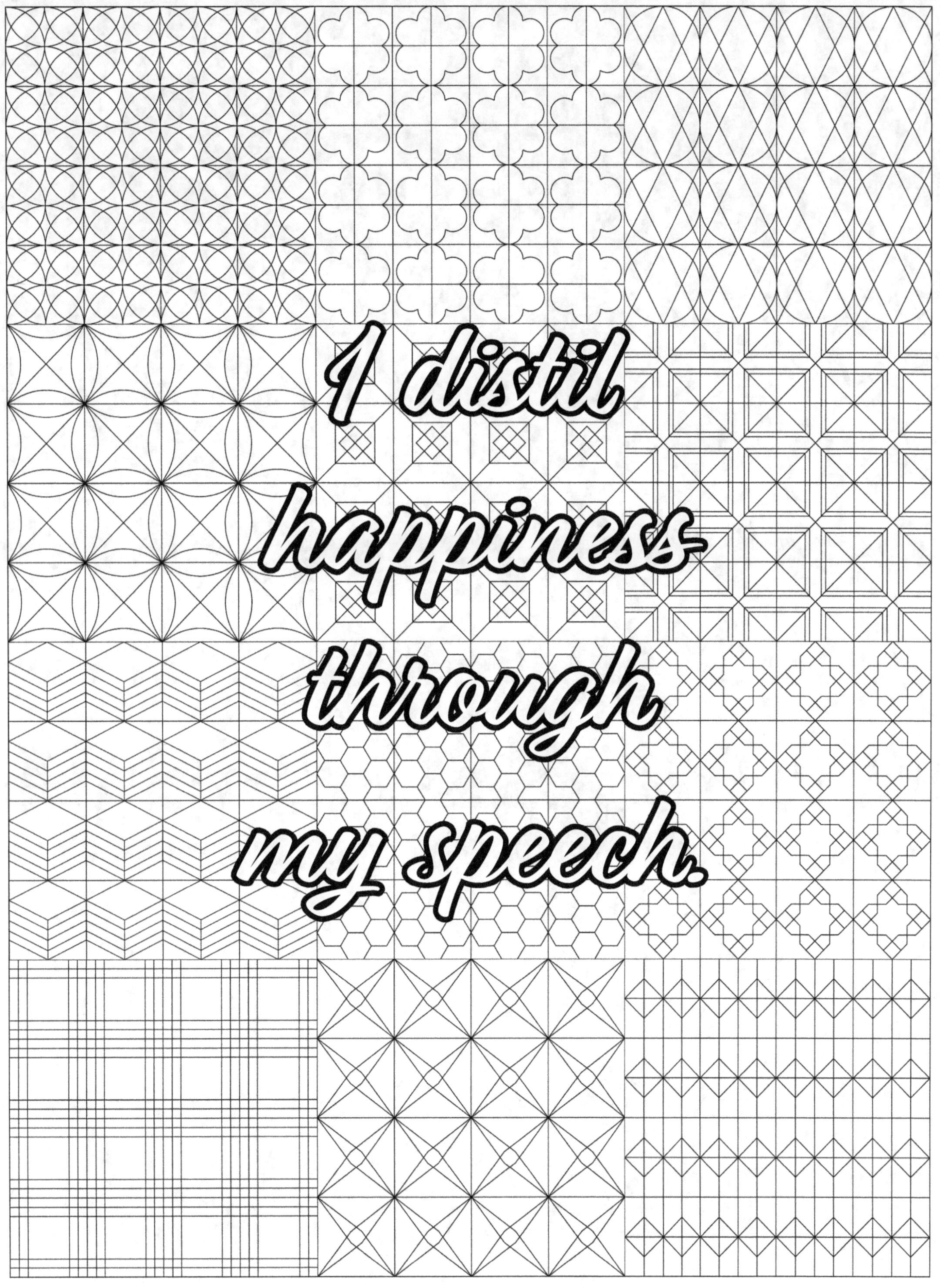
I distil
happiness
through
my speech.

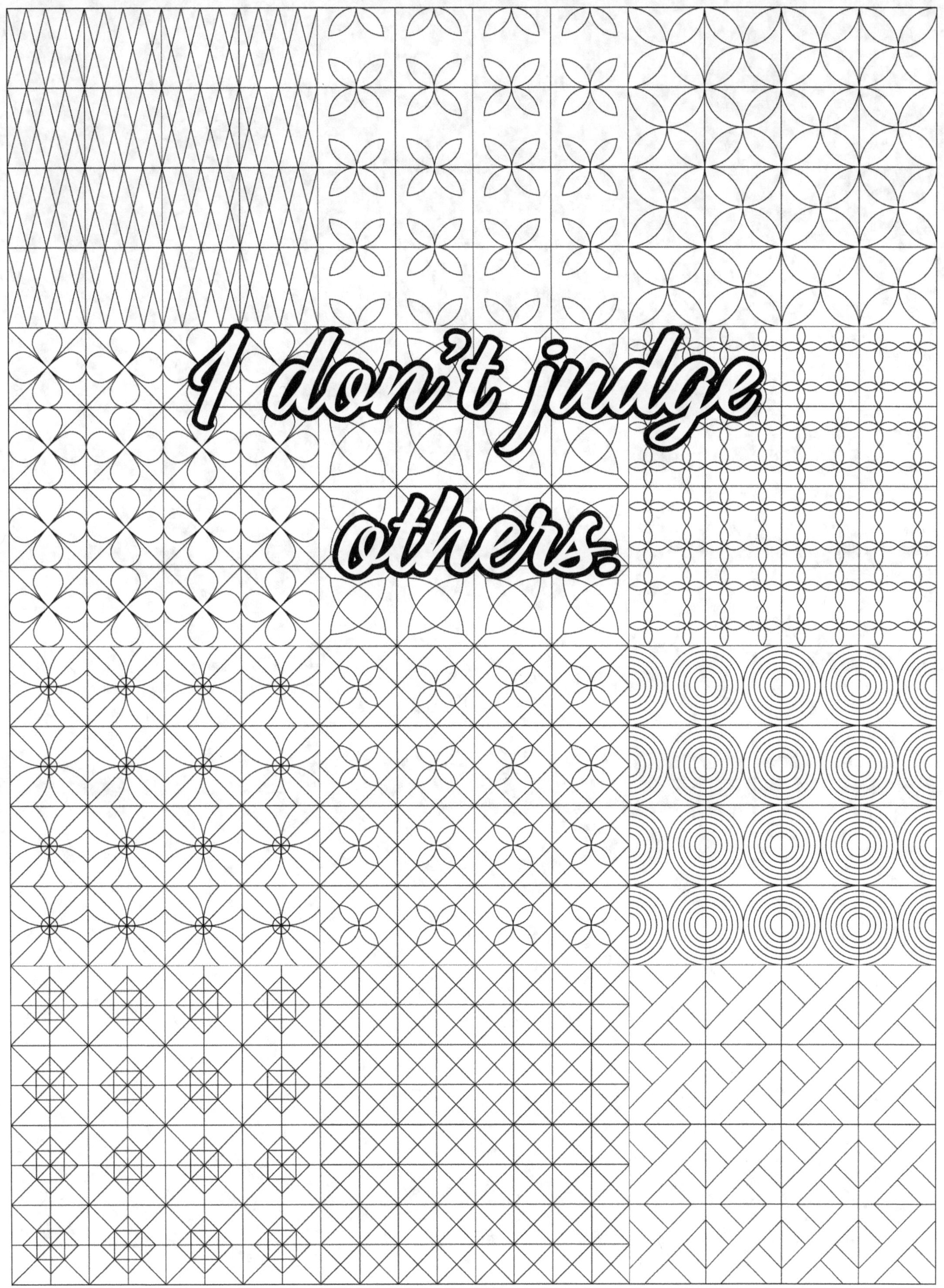
I don't judge others.

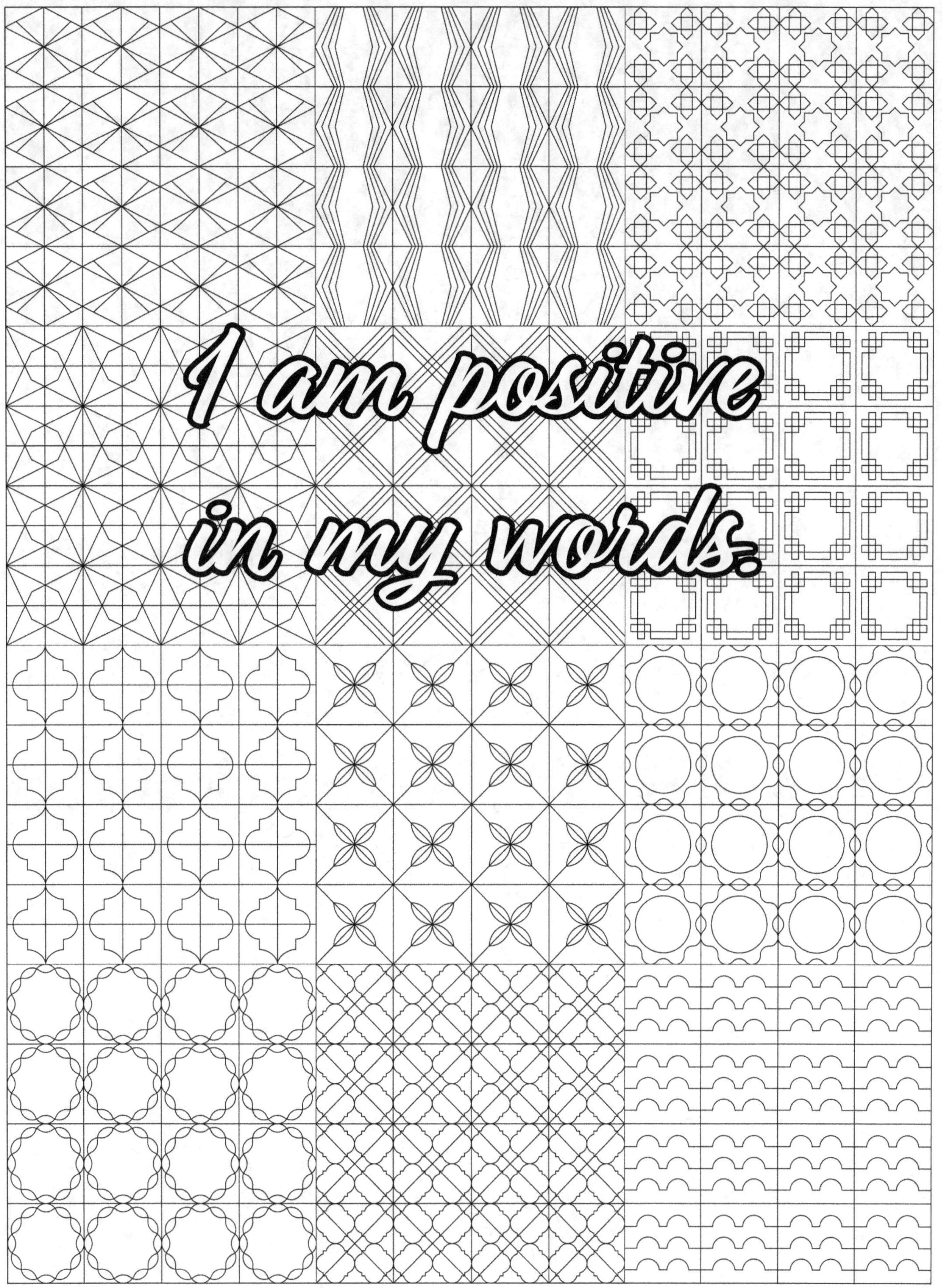
I am positive
in my words.

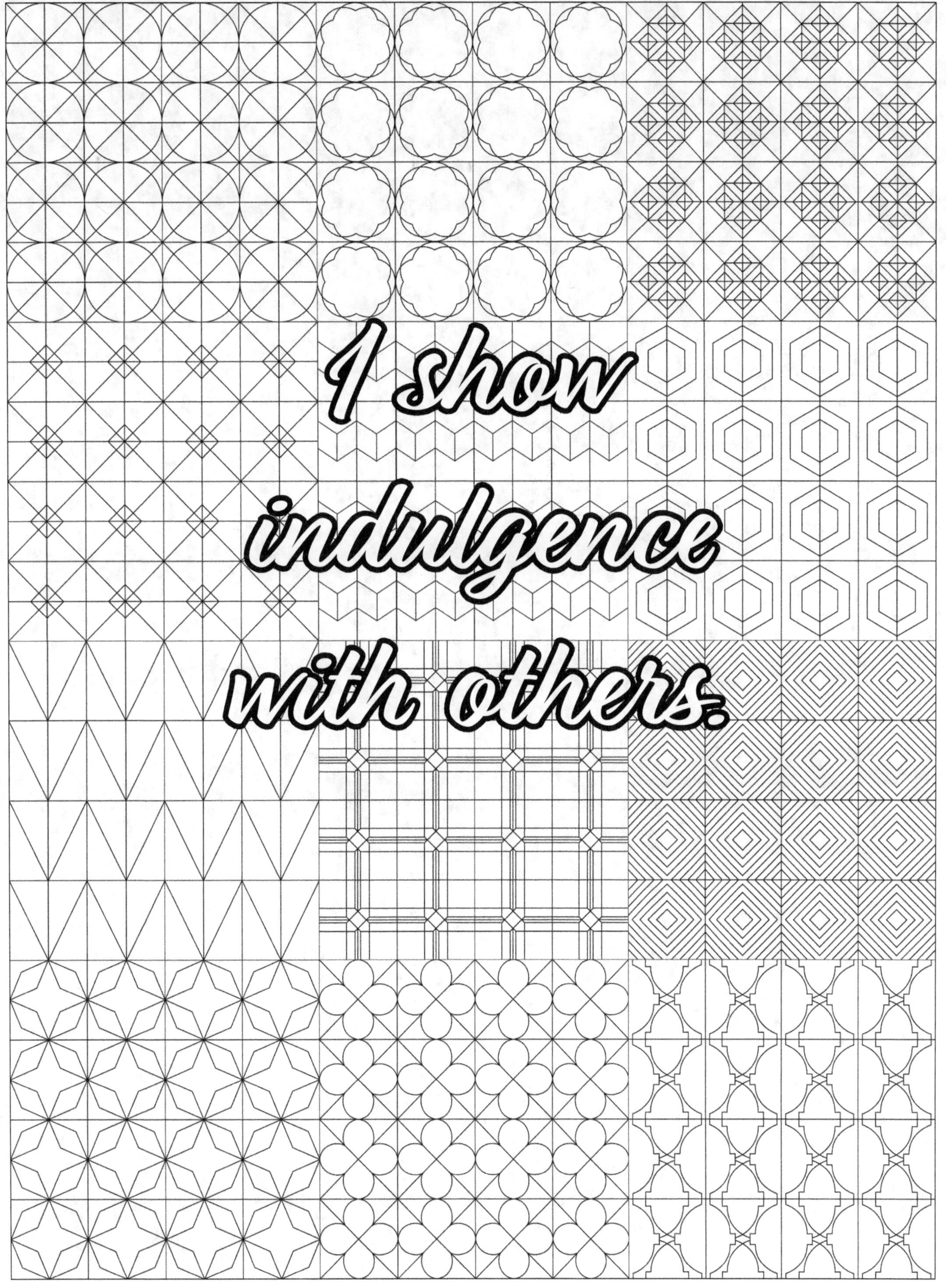
I show
indulgence
with others.

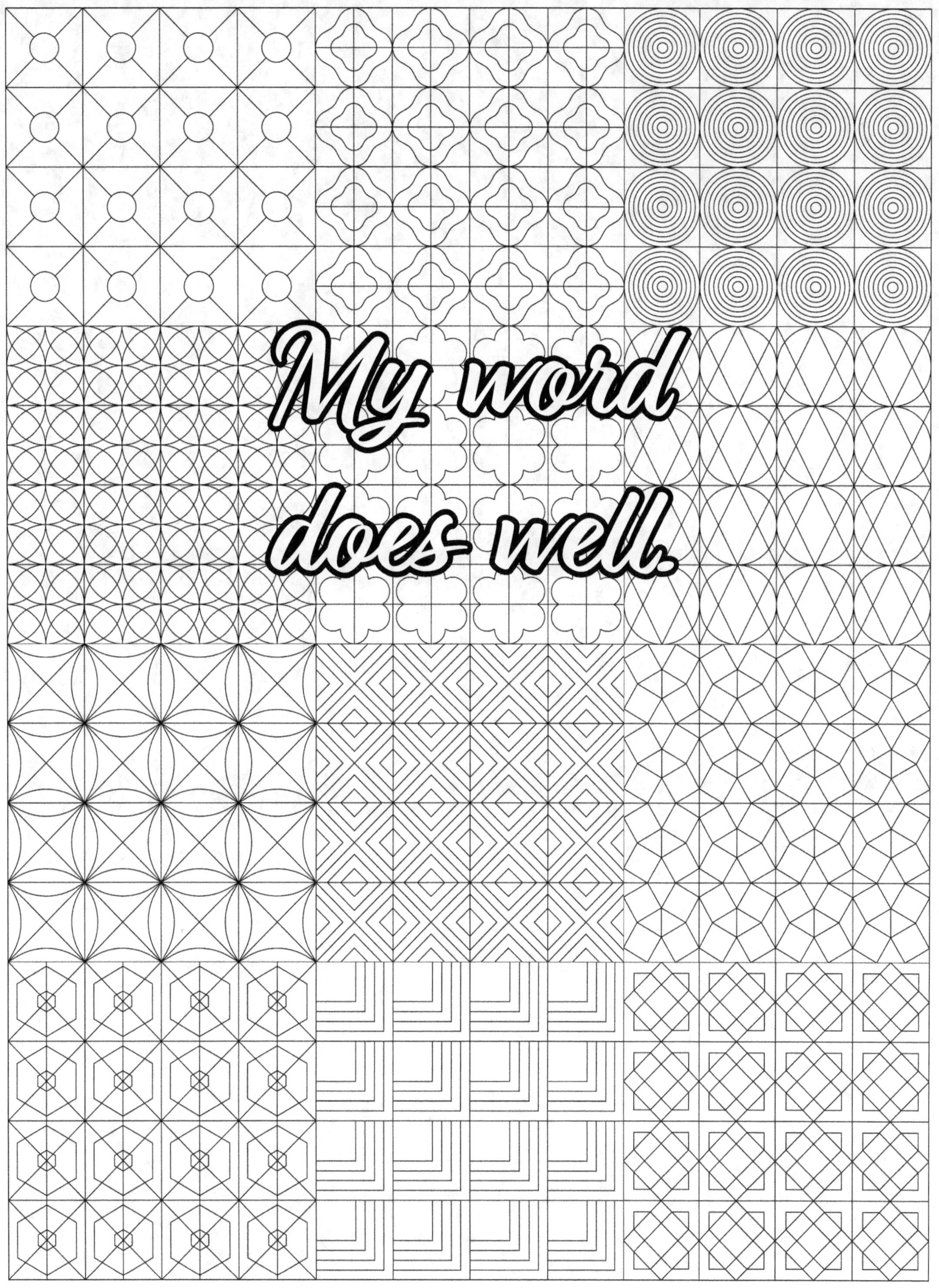
My word
does well.

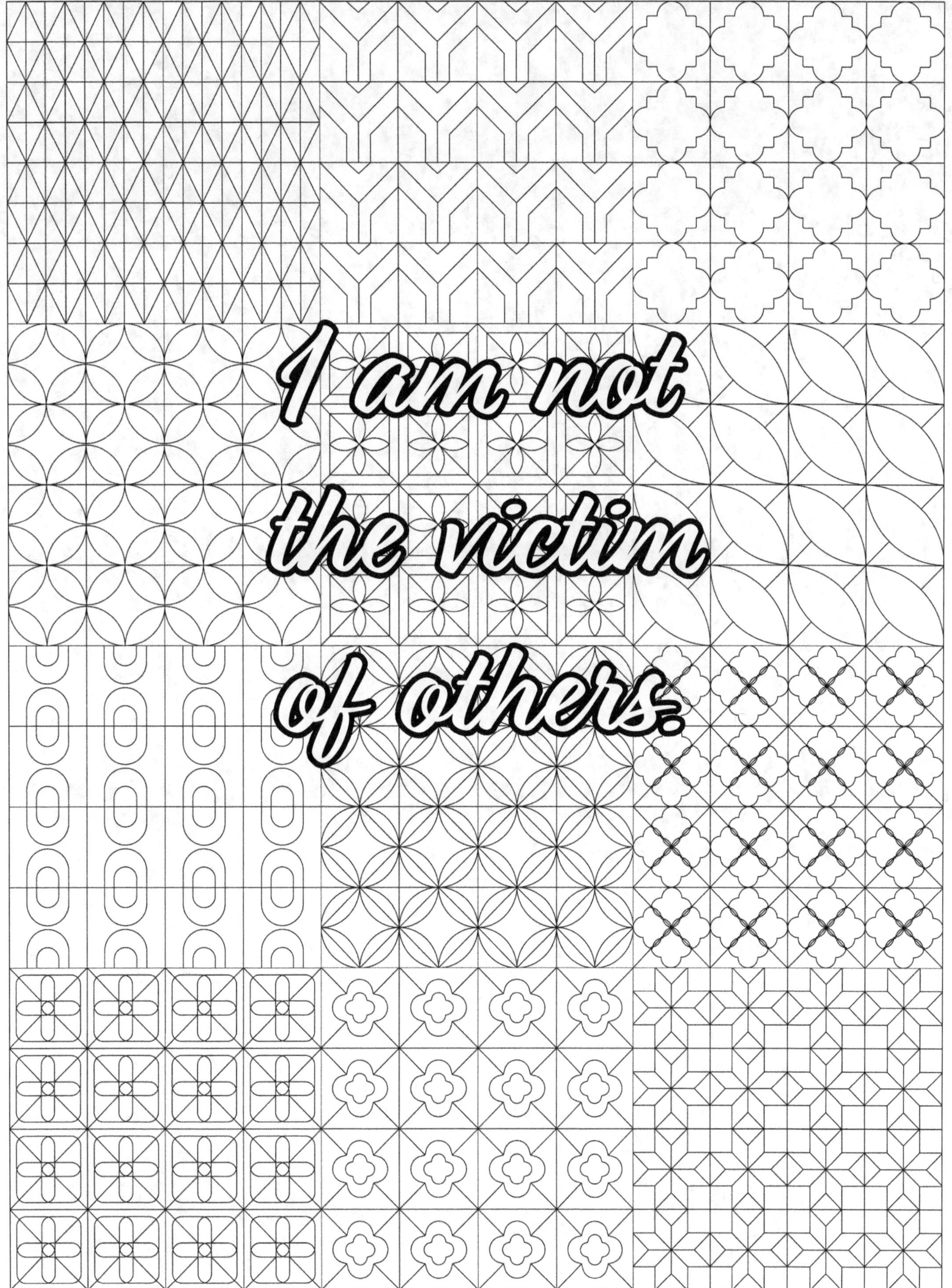
I am not
the victim
of others.

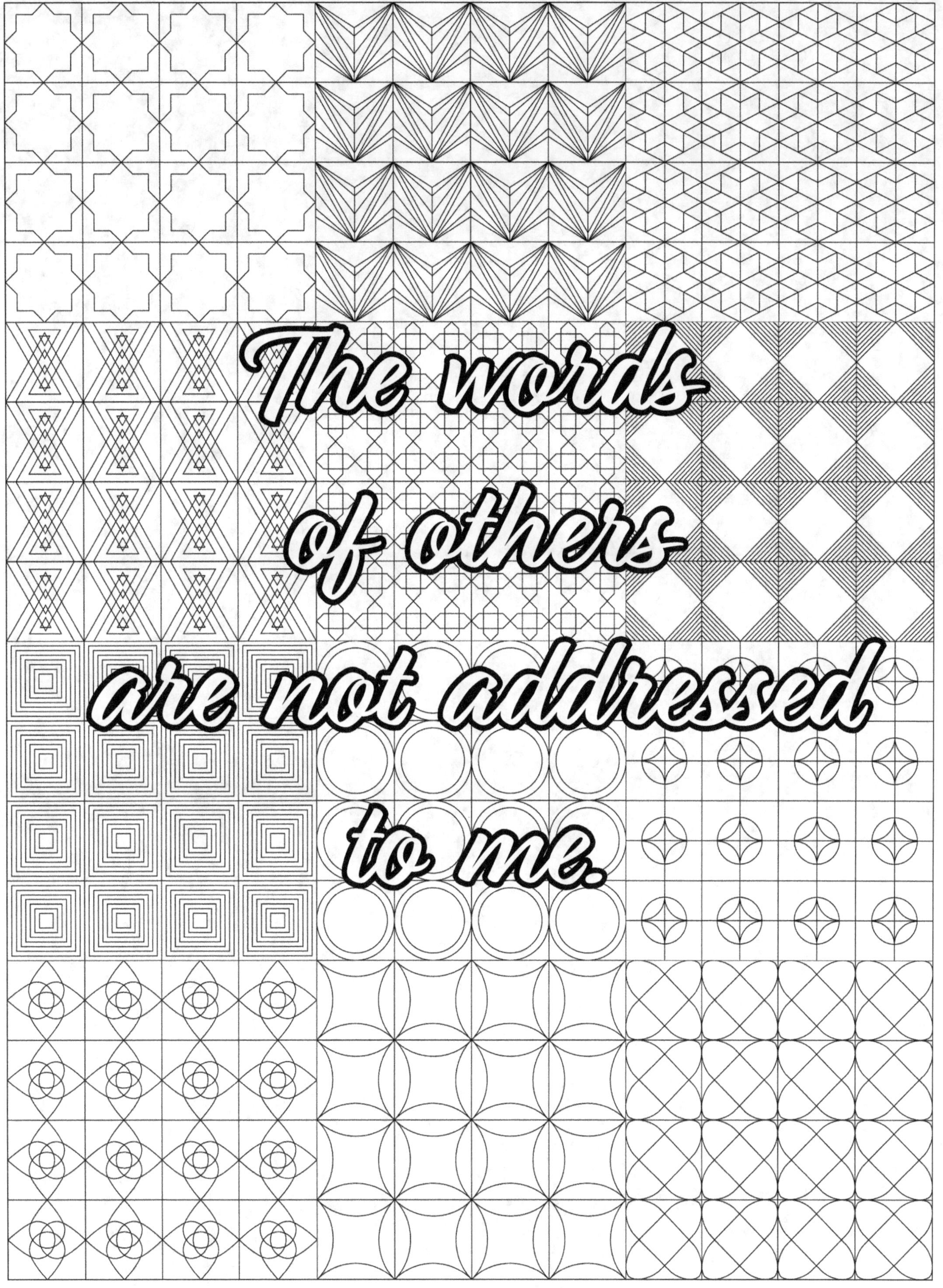

The words
of others
are not addressed
to me.

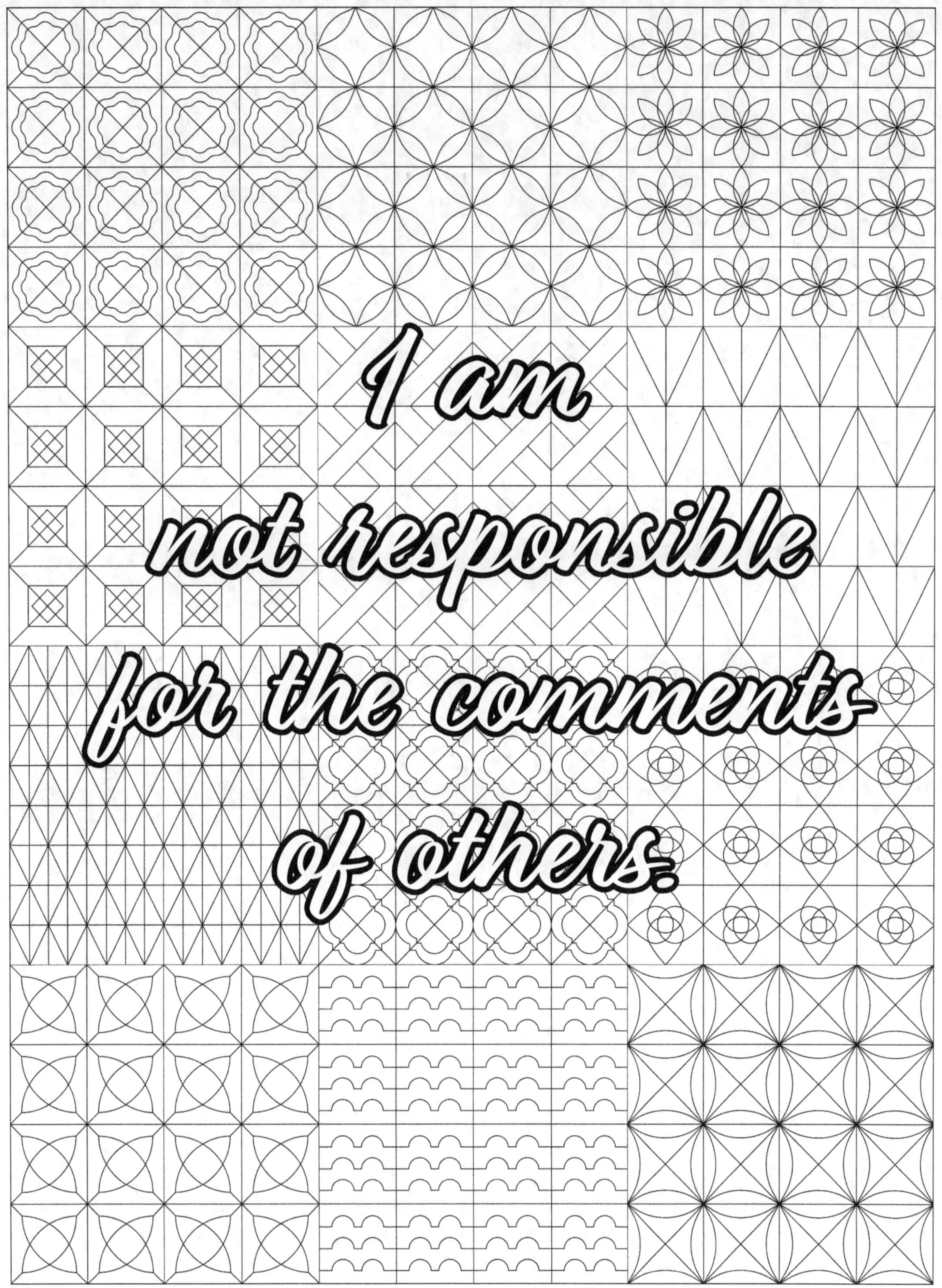

I am
not responsible
for the comments
of others.

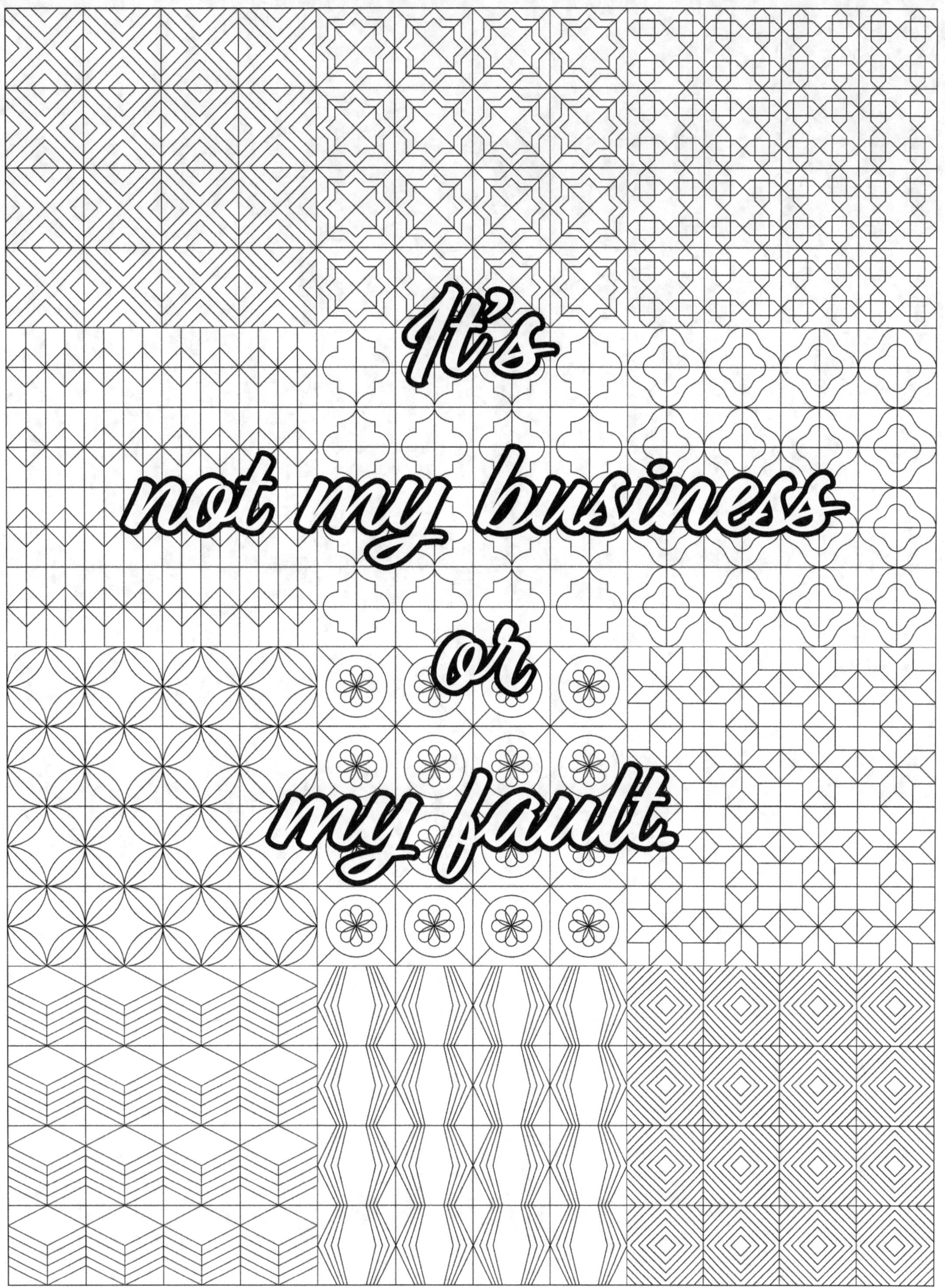
It's
not my business
or
my fault.

I take
a step back
from what
other people say.

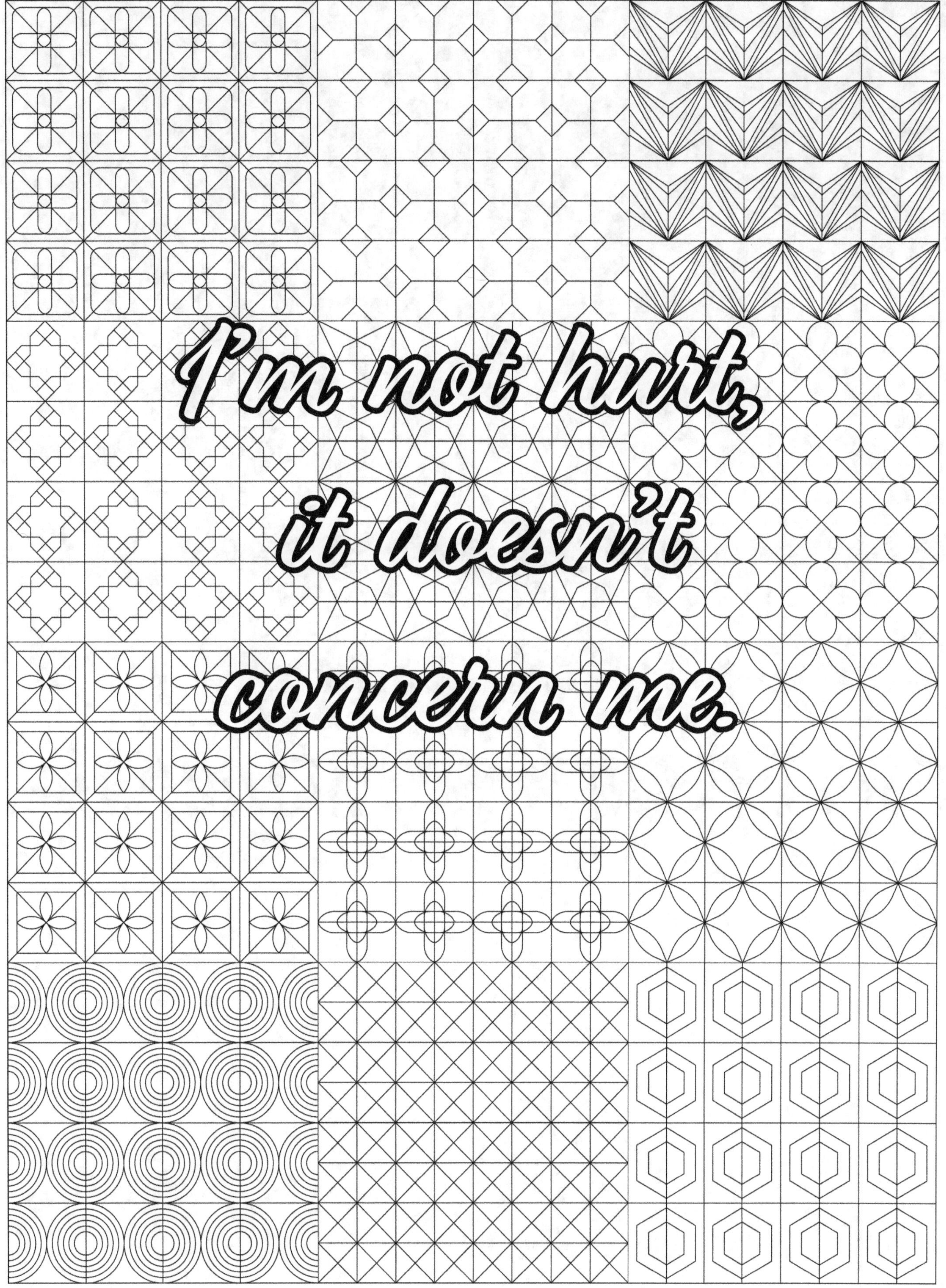
I'm not hurt, it doesn't concern me.

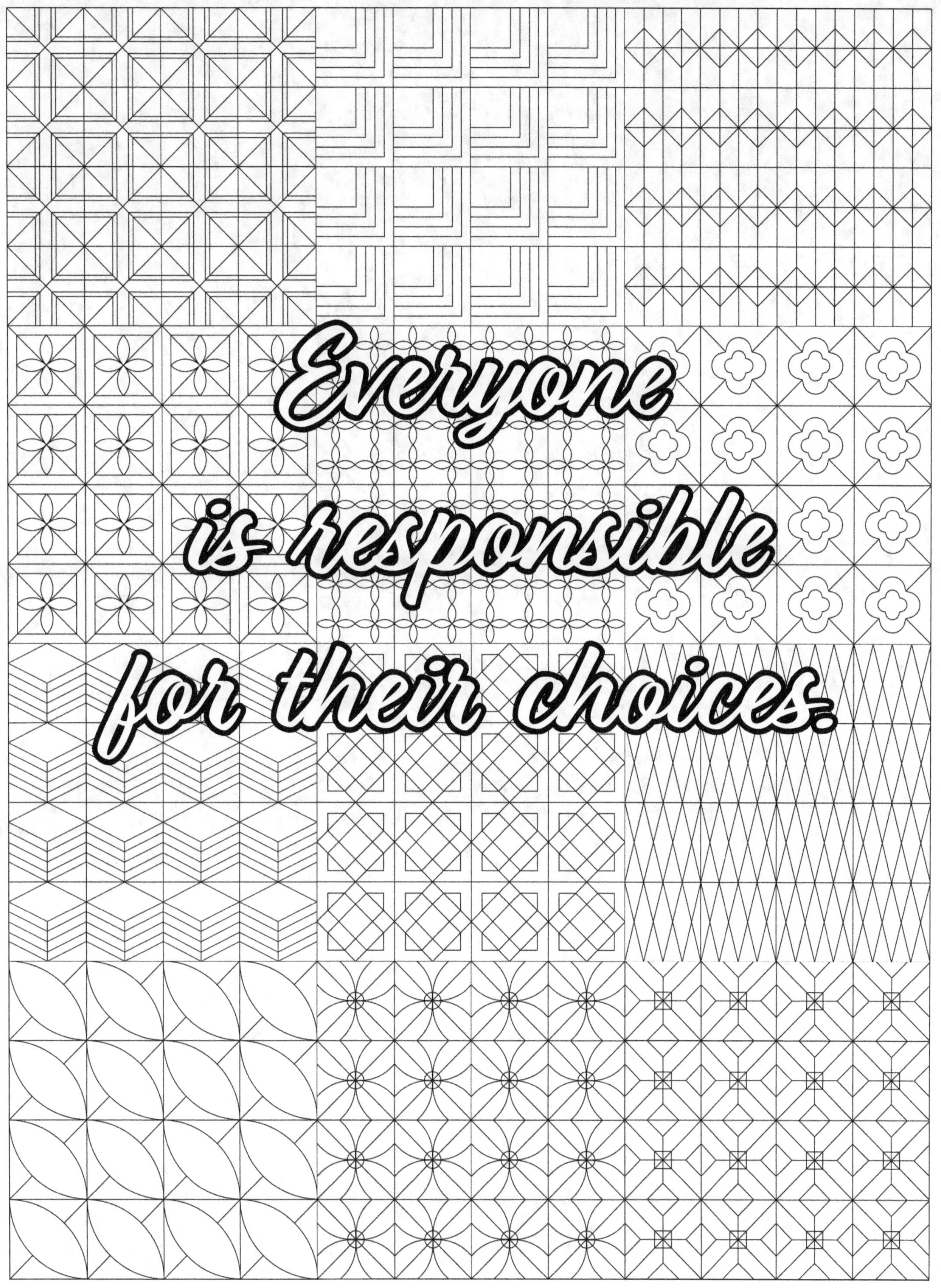
Everyone
is responsible
for their choices.

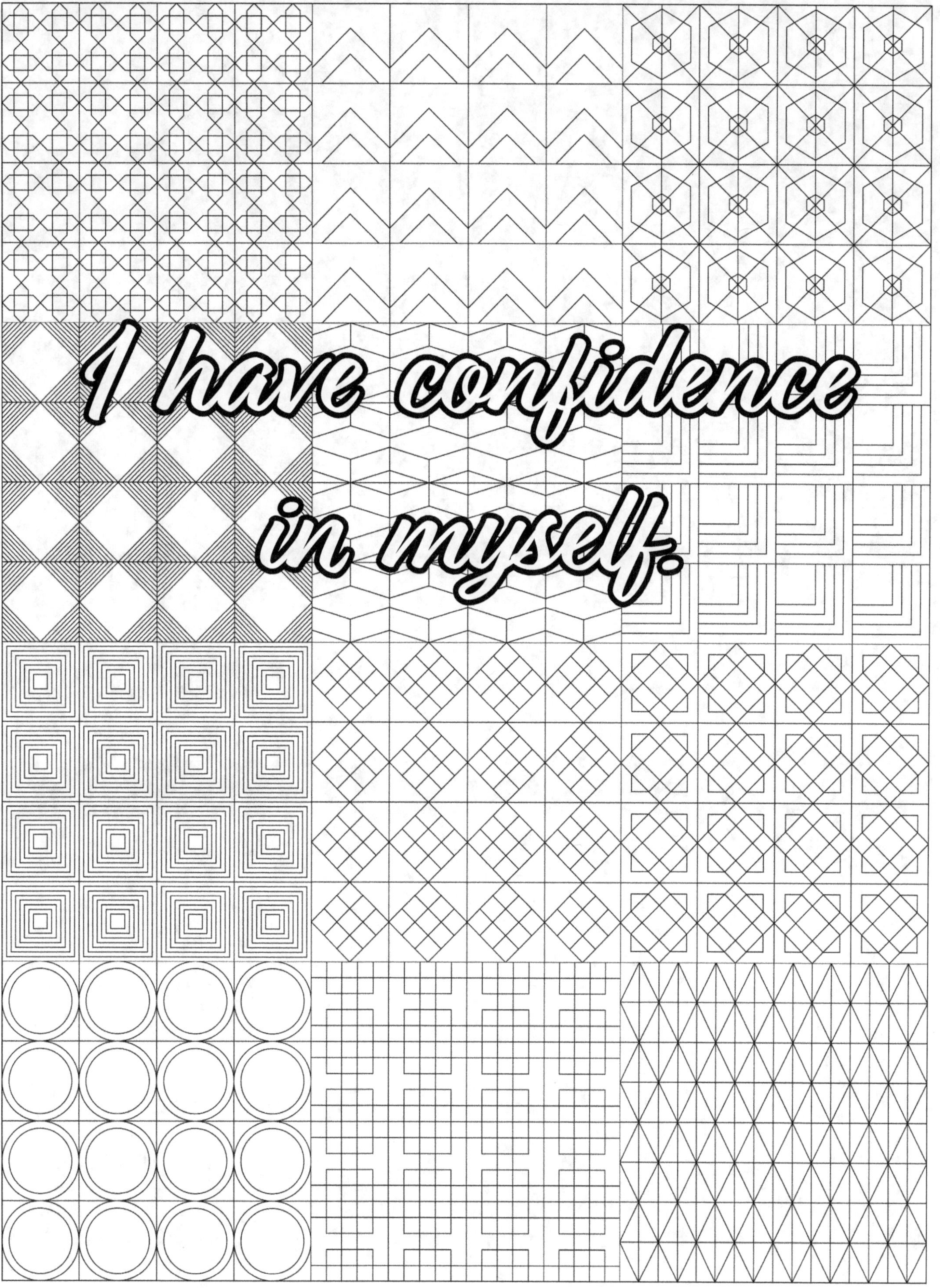
I have confidence
in myself.

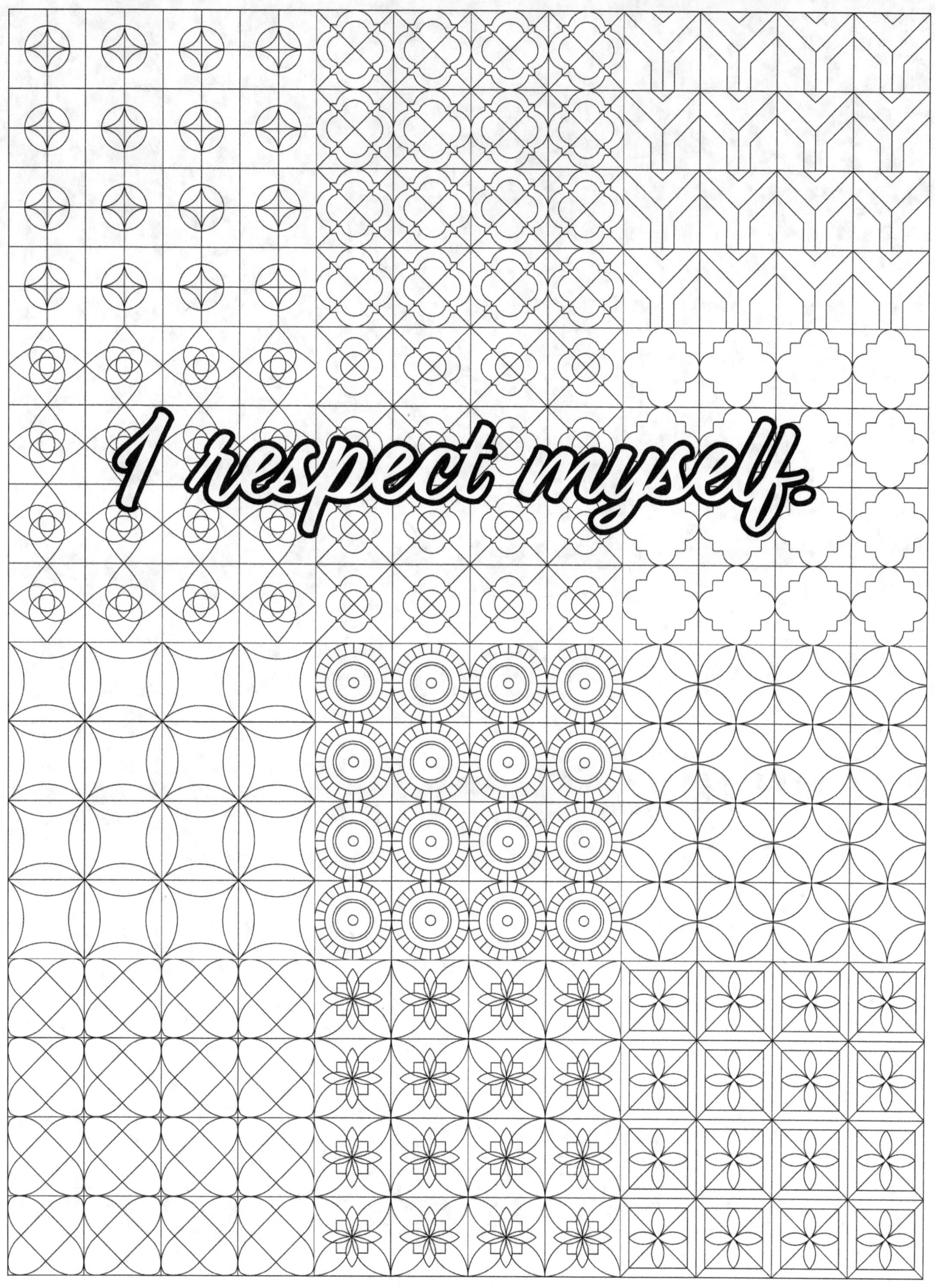
I respect myself.

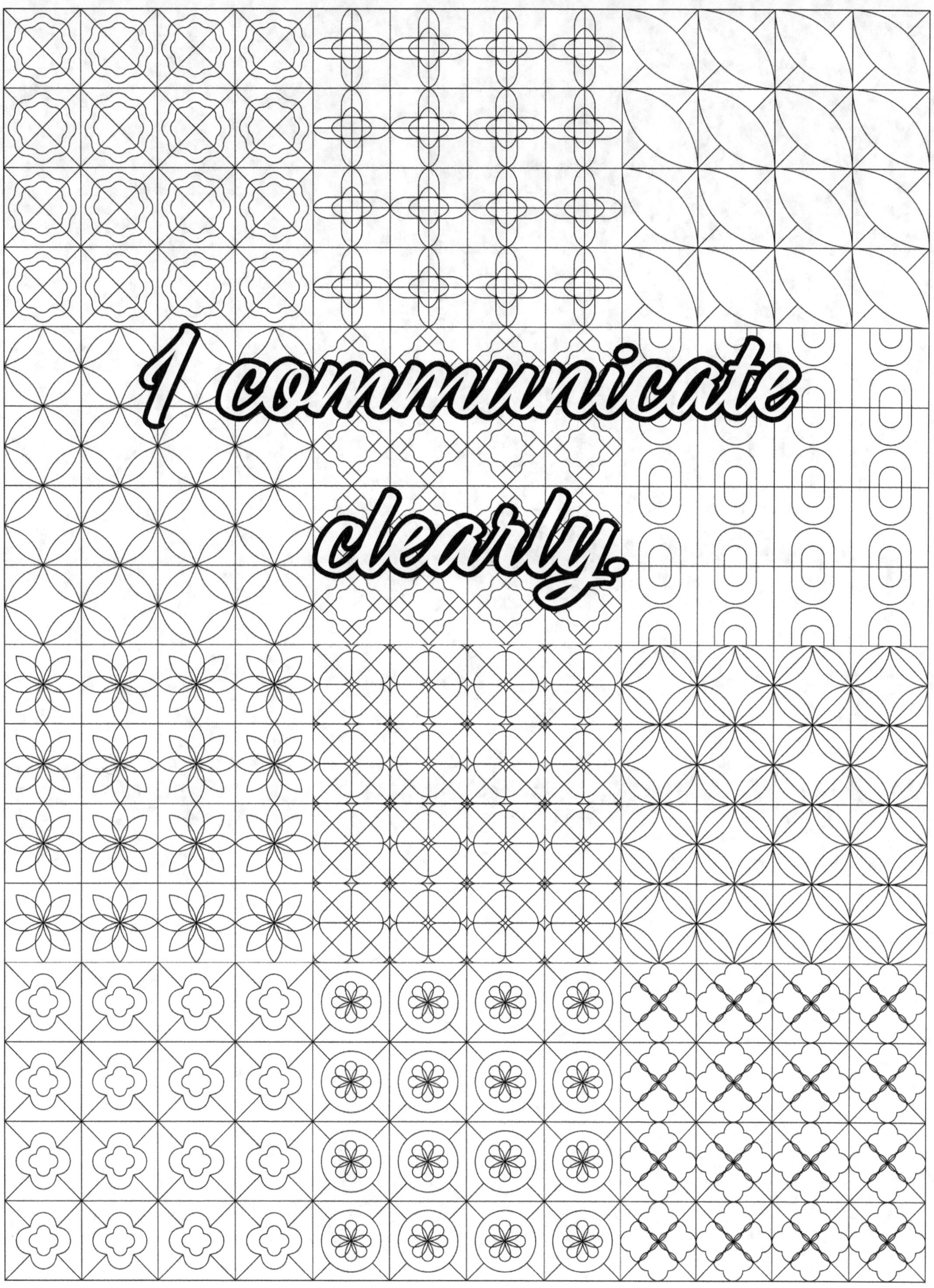
I communicate clearly.

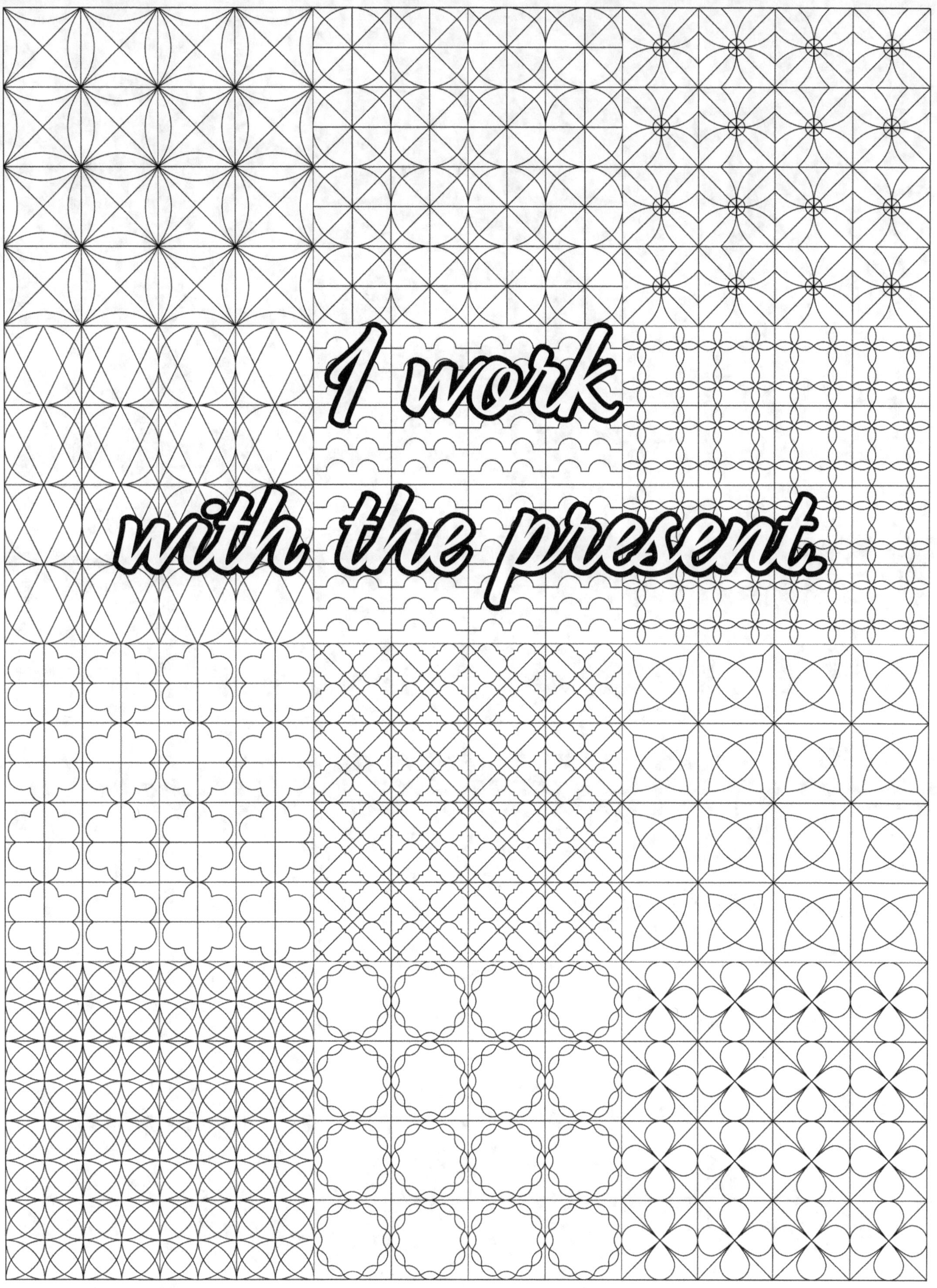
I work
with the present.

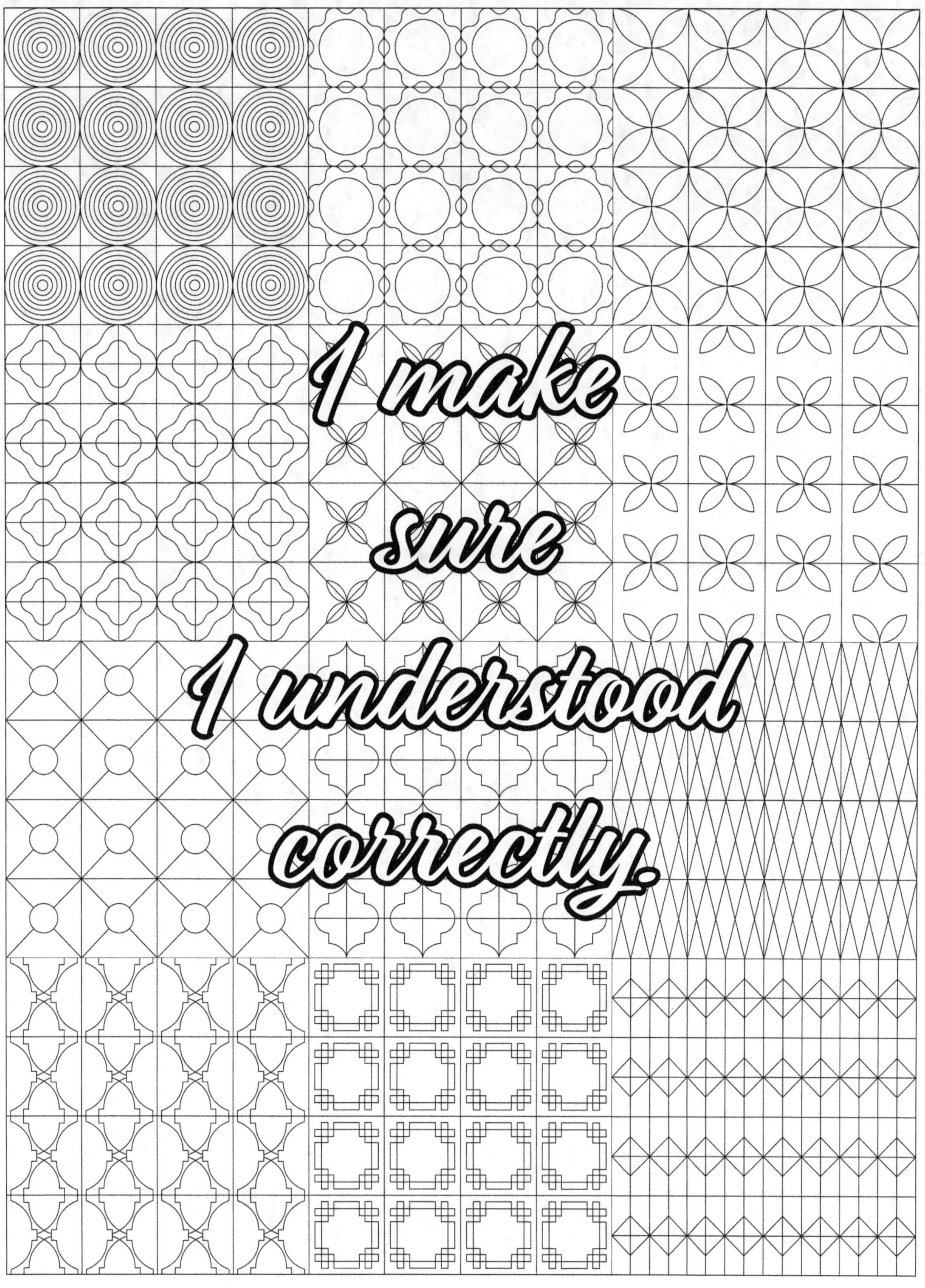
I make
sure
I understood
correctly.

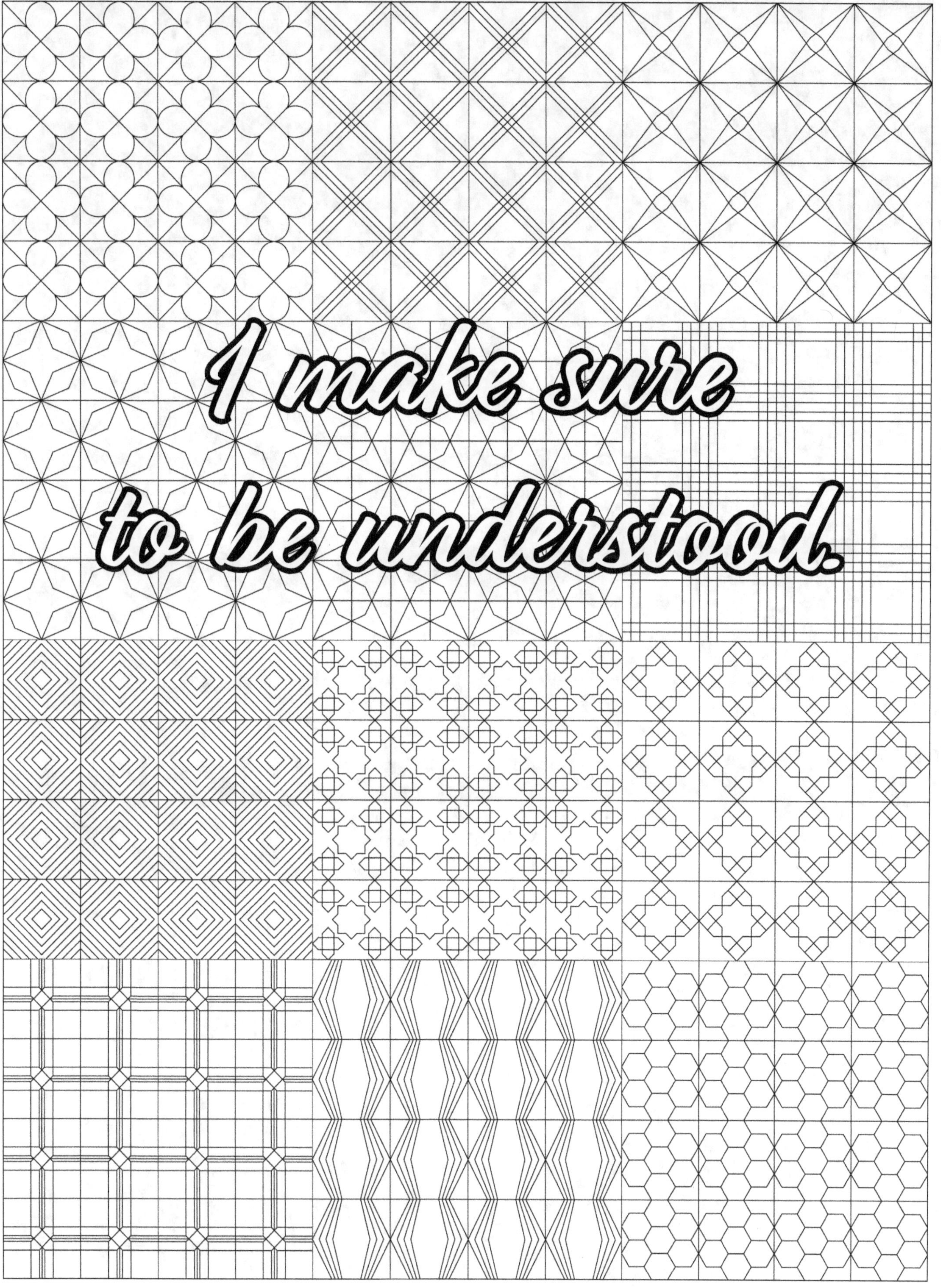
I make sure
to be understood.

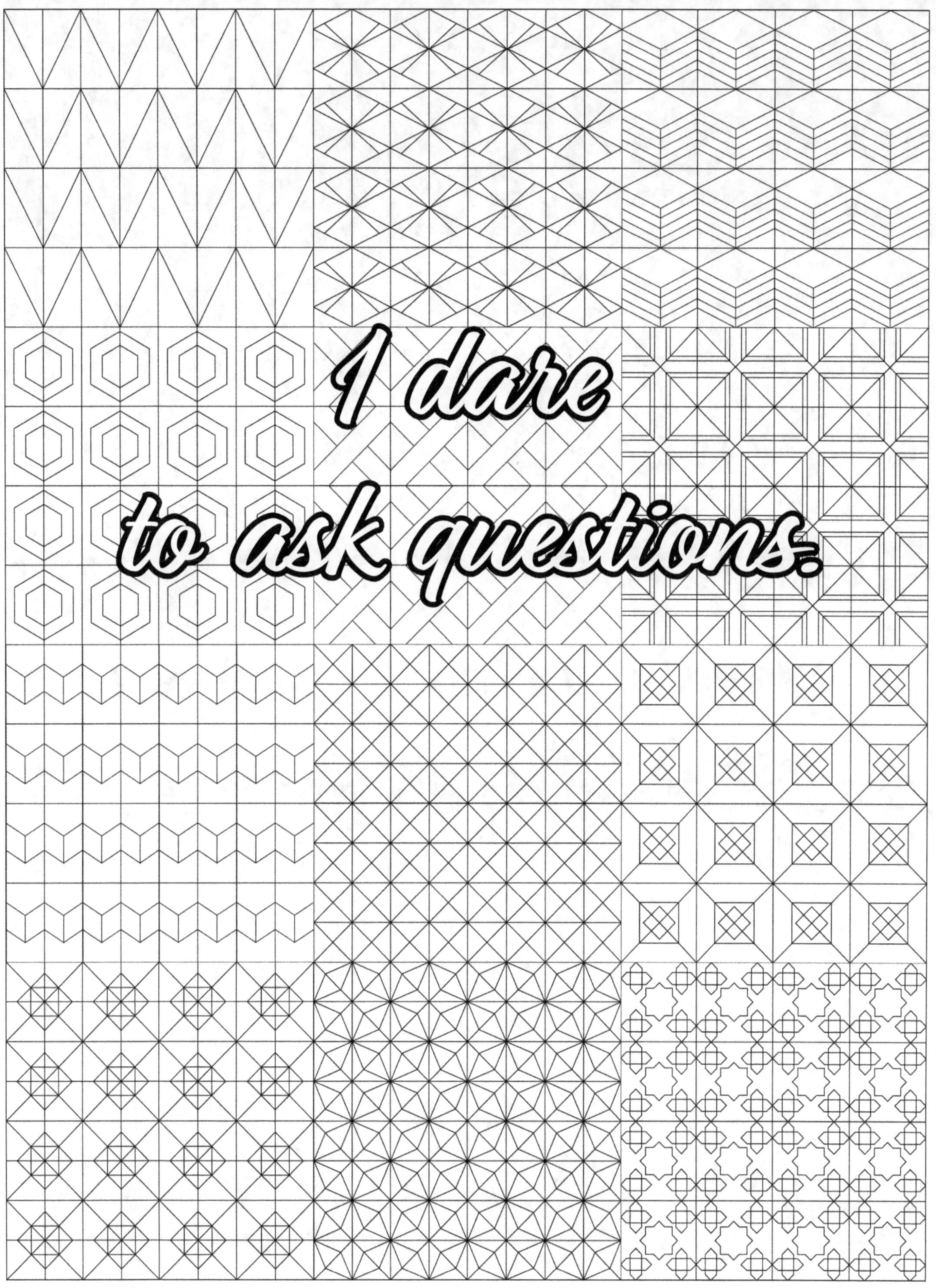
I dare
to ask questions.

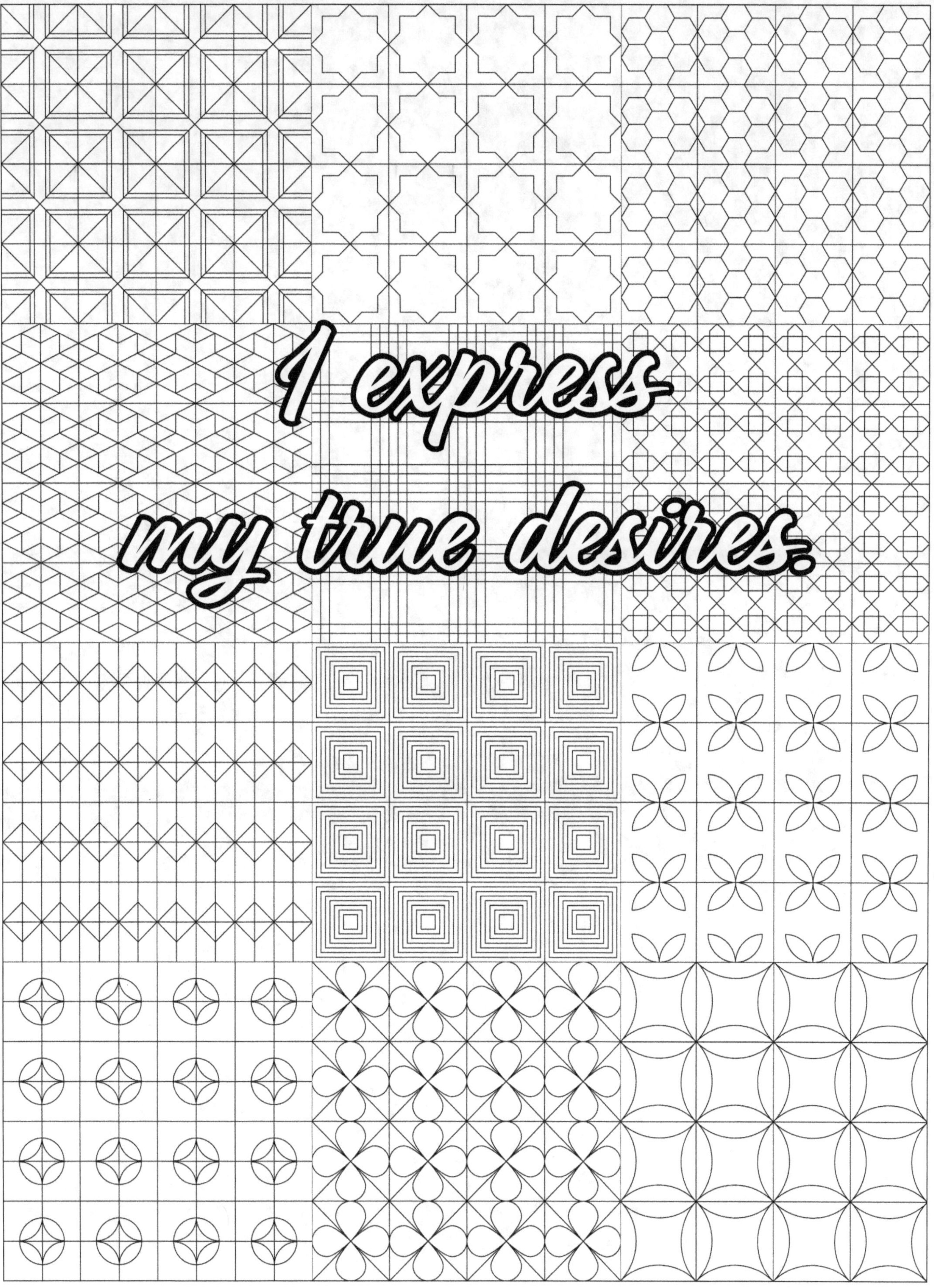

I express
my true desires.

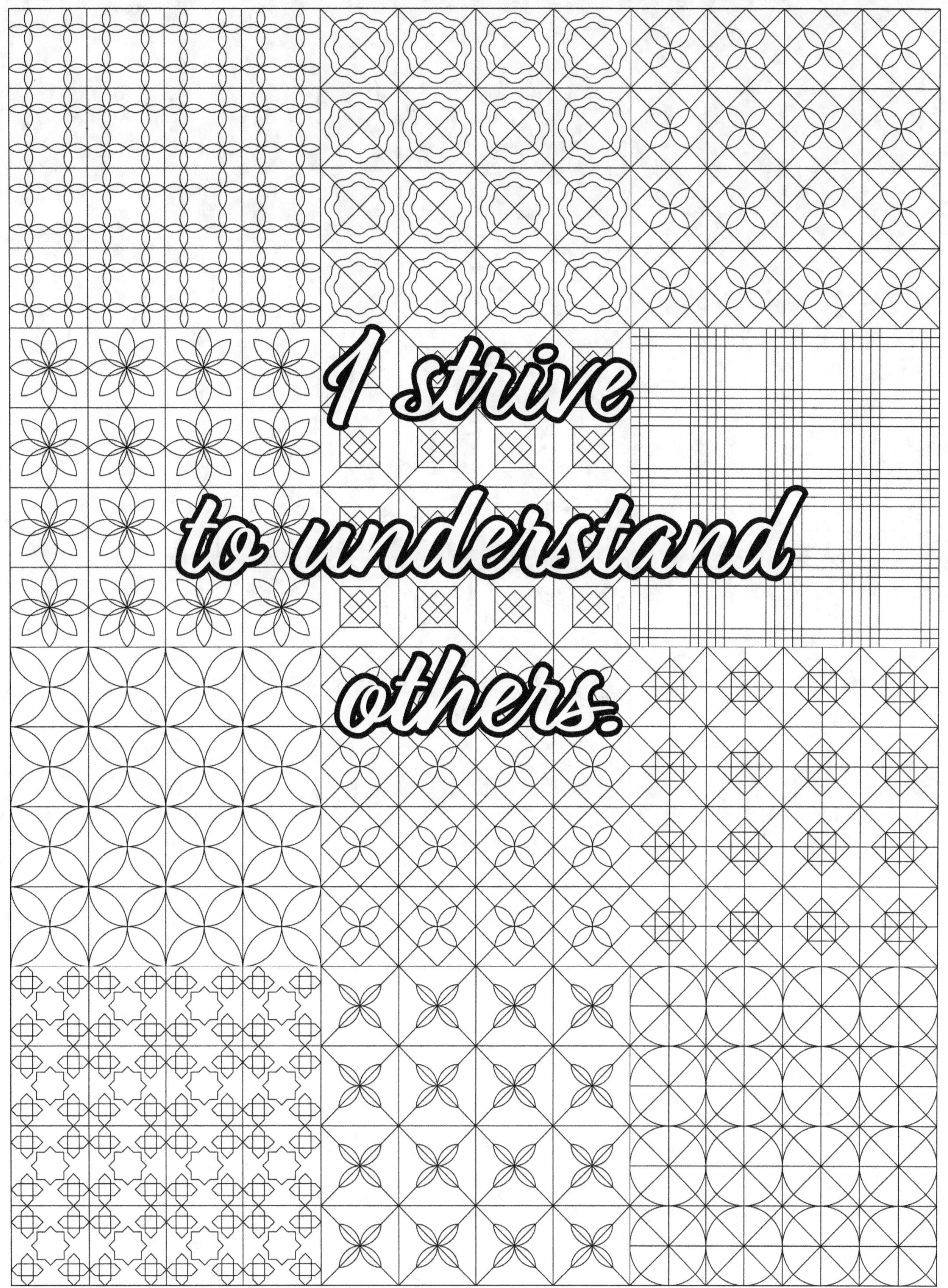
I strive
to understand
others.

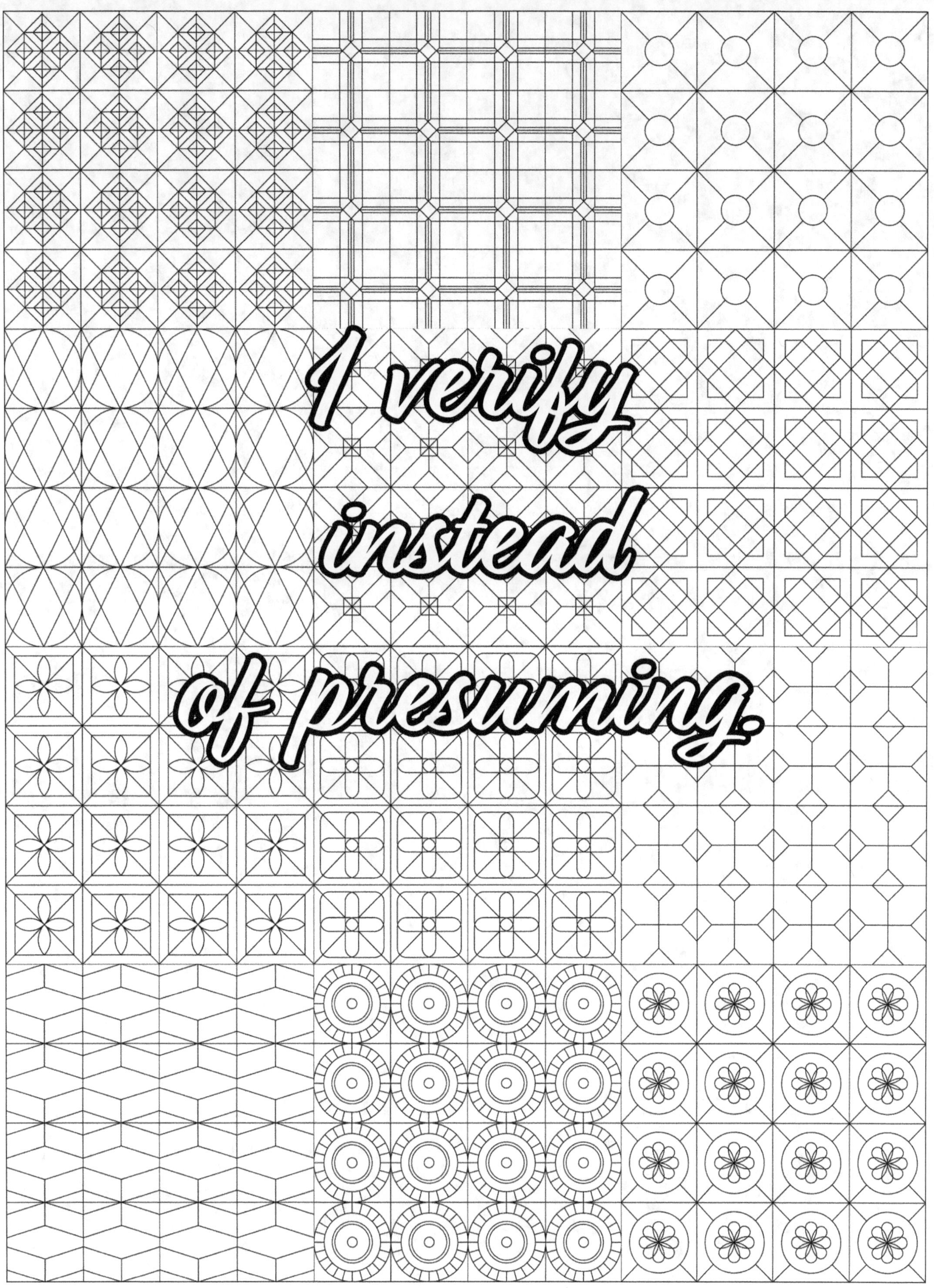

I verify
instead
of presuming.

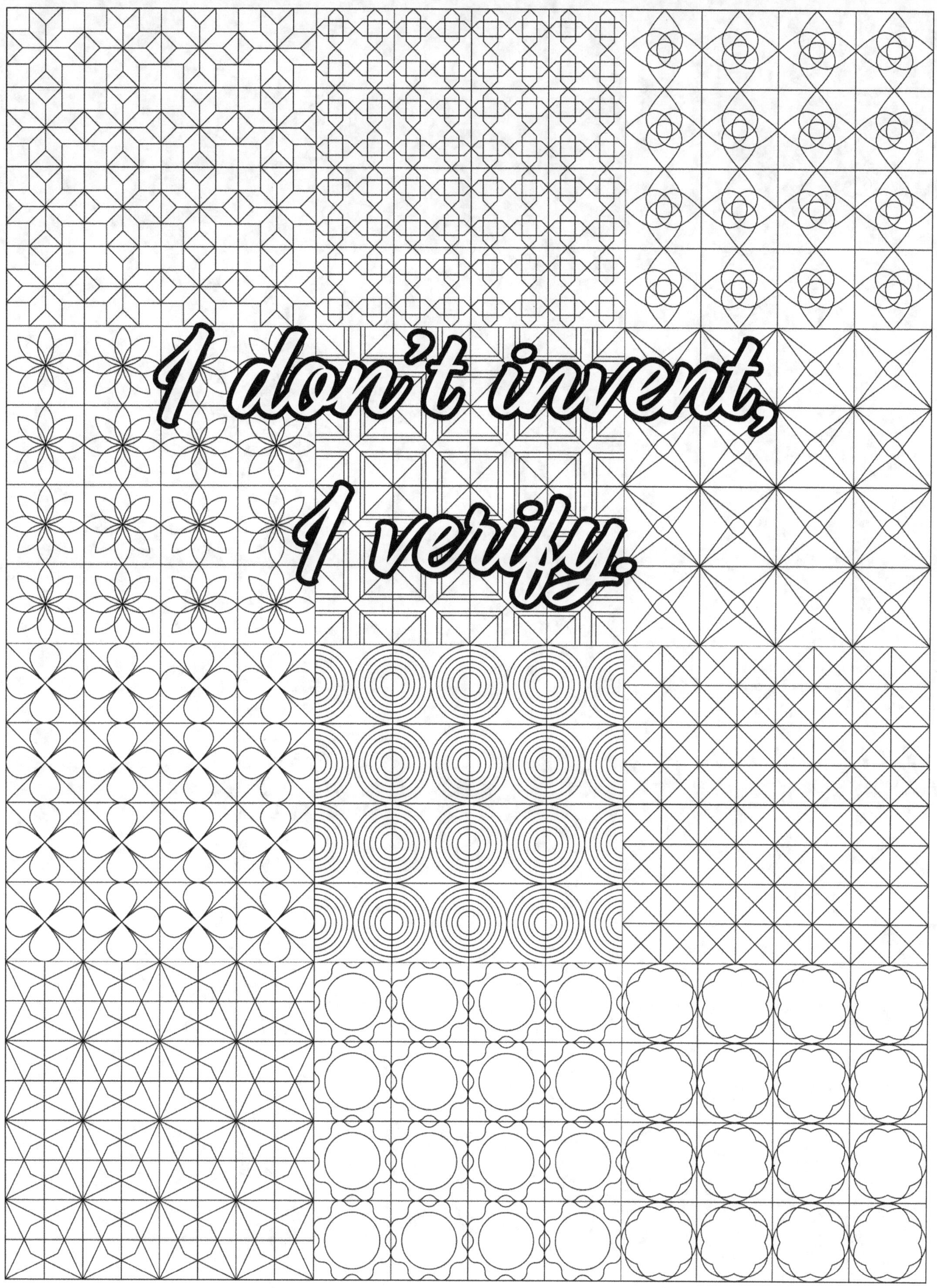

I don't invent,
I verify.

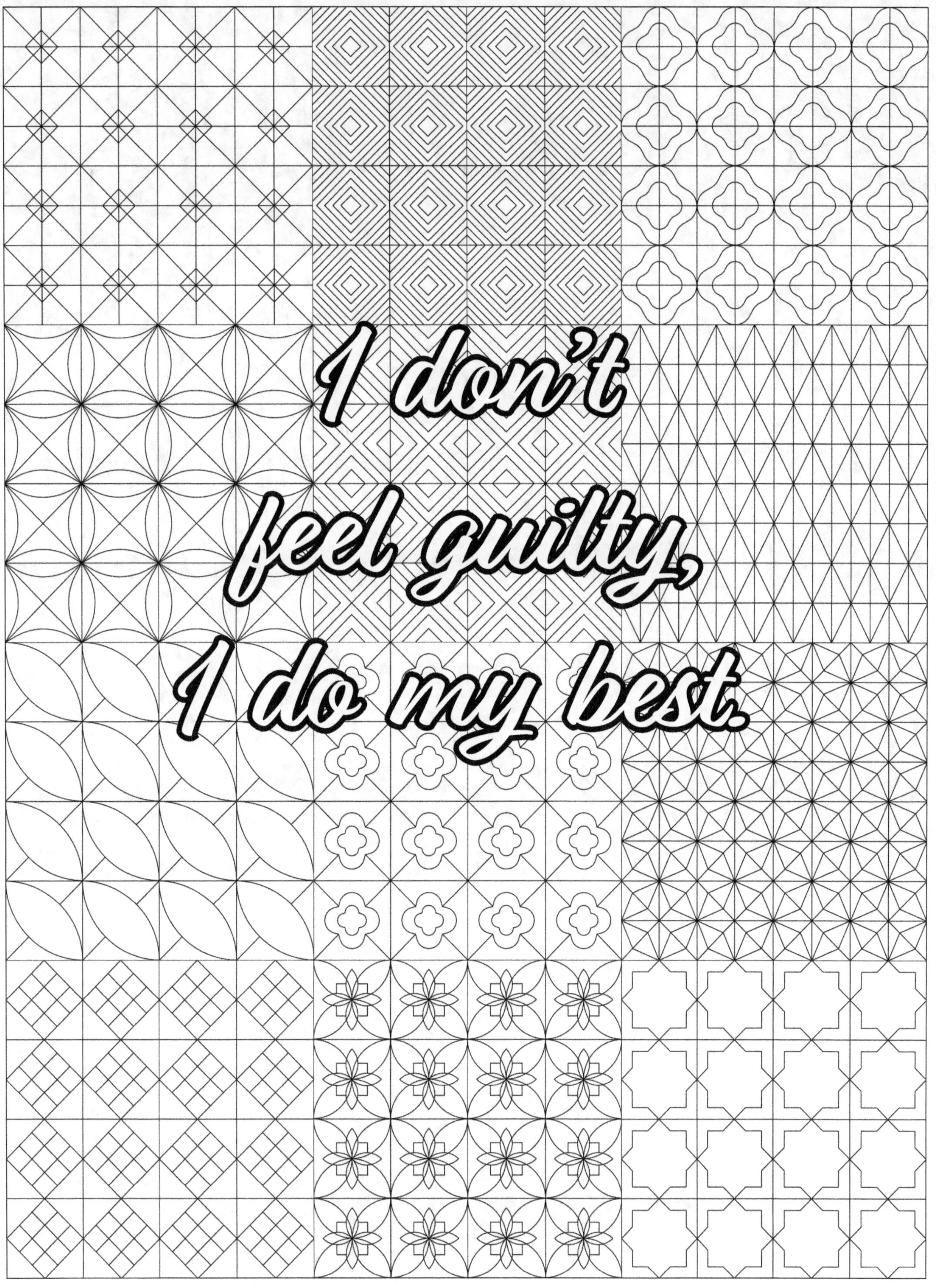
I don't
feel guilty,
I do my best.

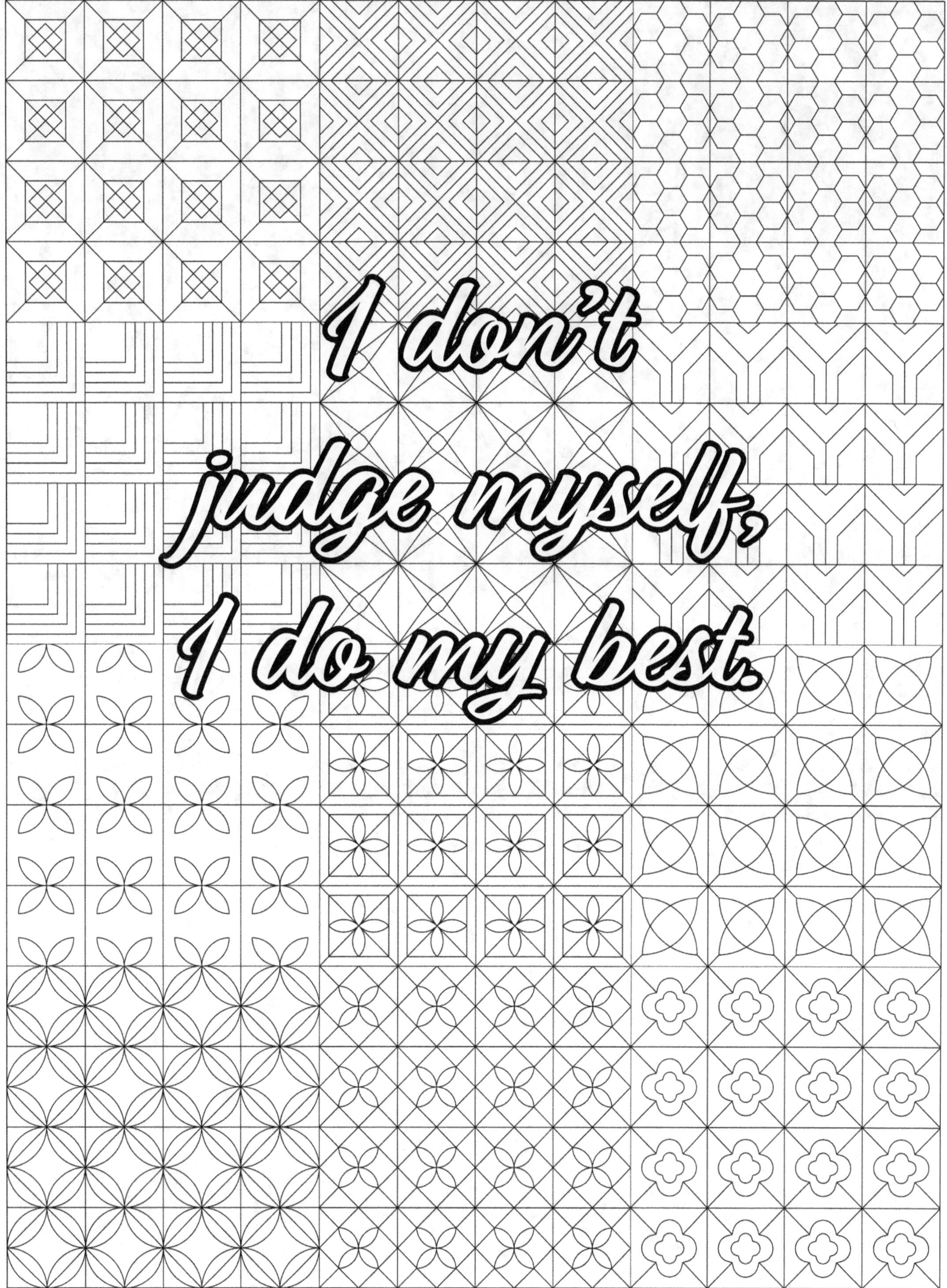

I don't
judge myself,
I do my best.

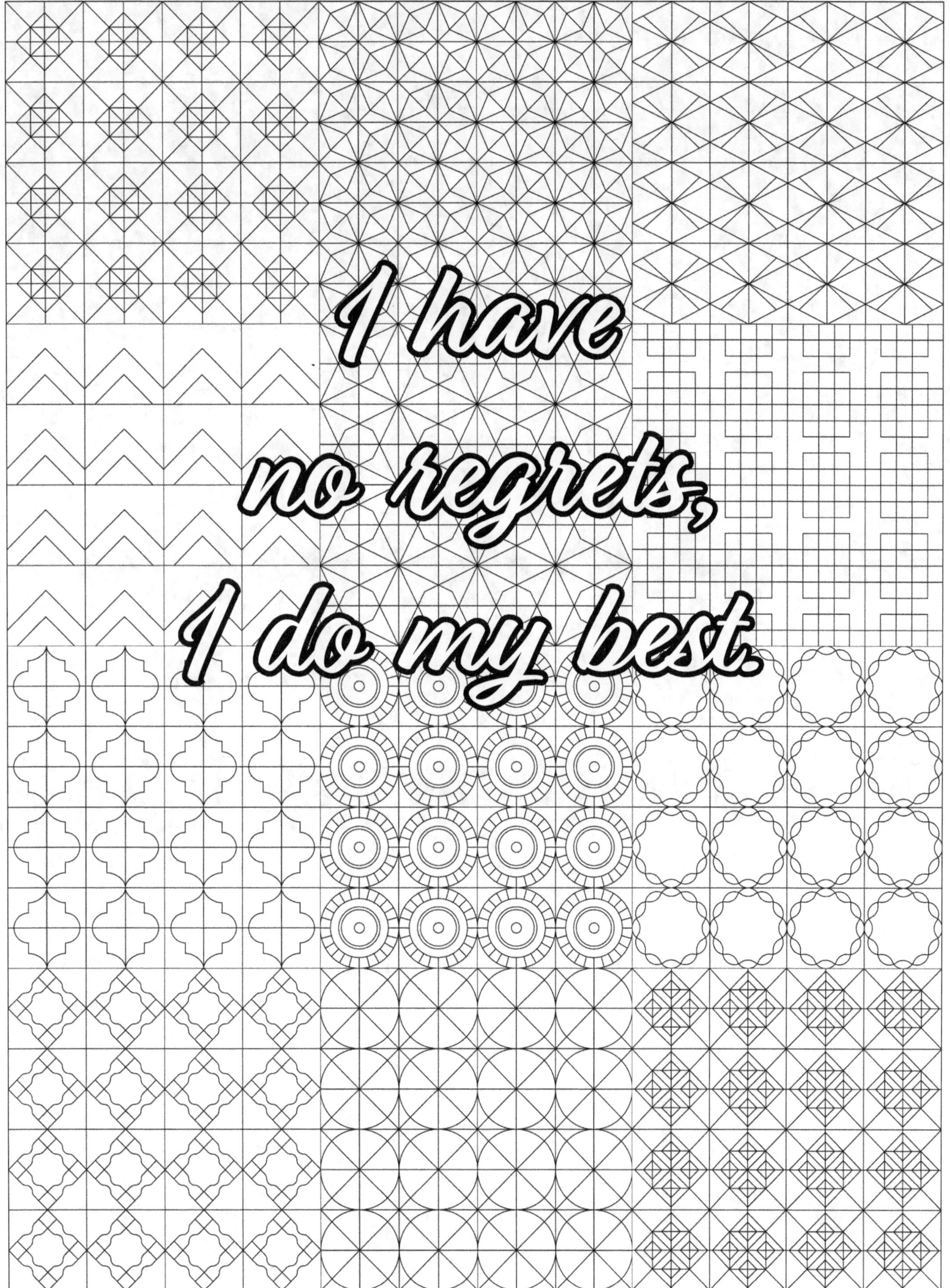

I have
no regrets,
I do my best.

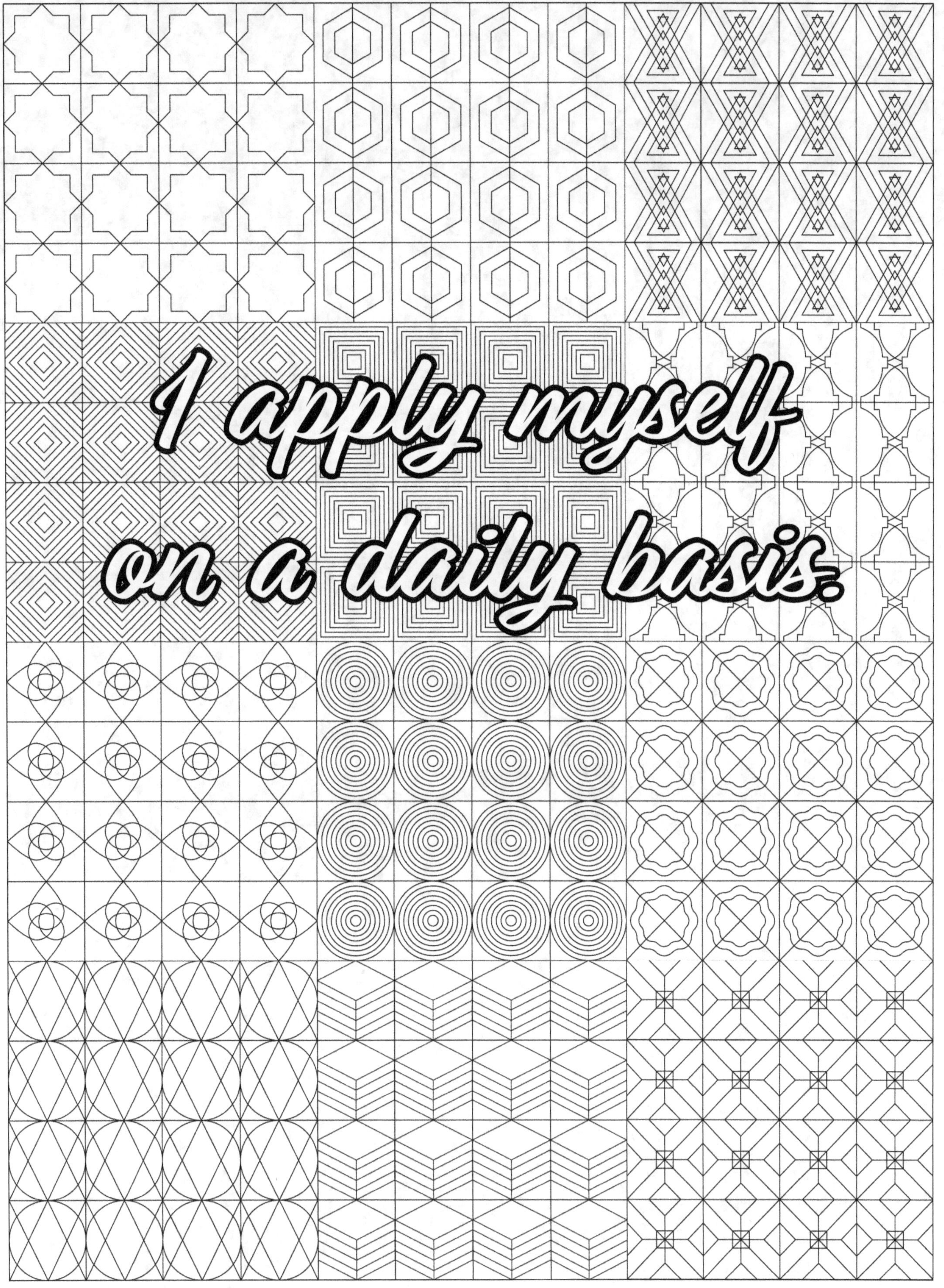

I apply myself
on a daily basis.

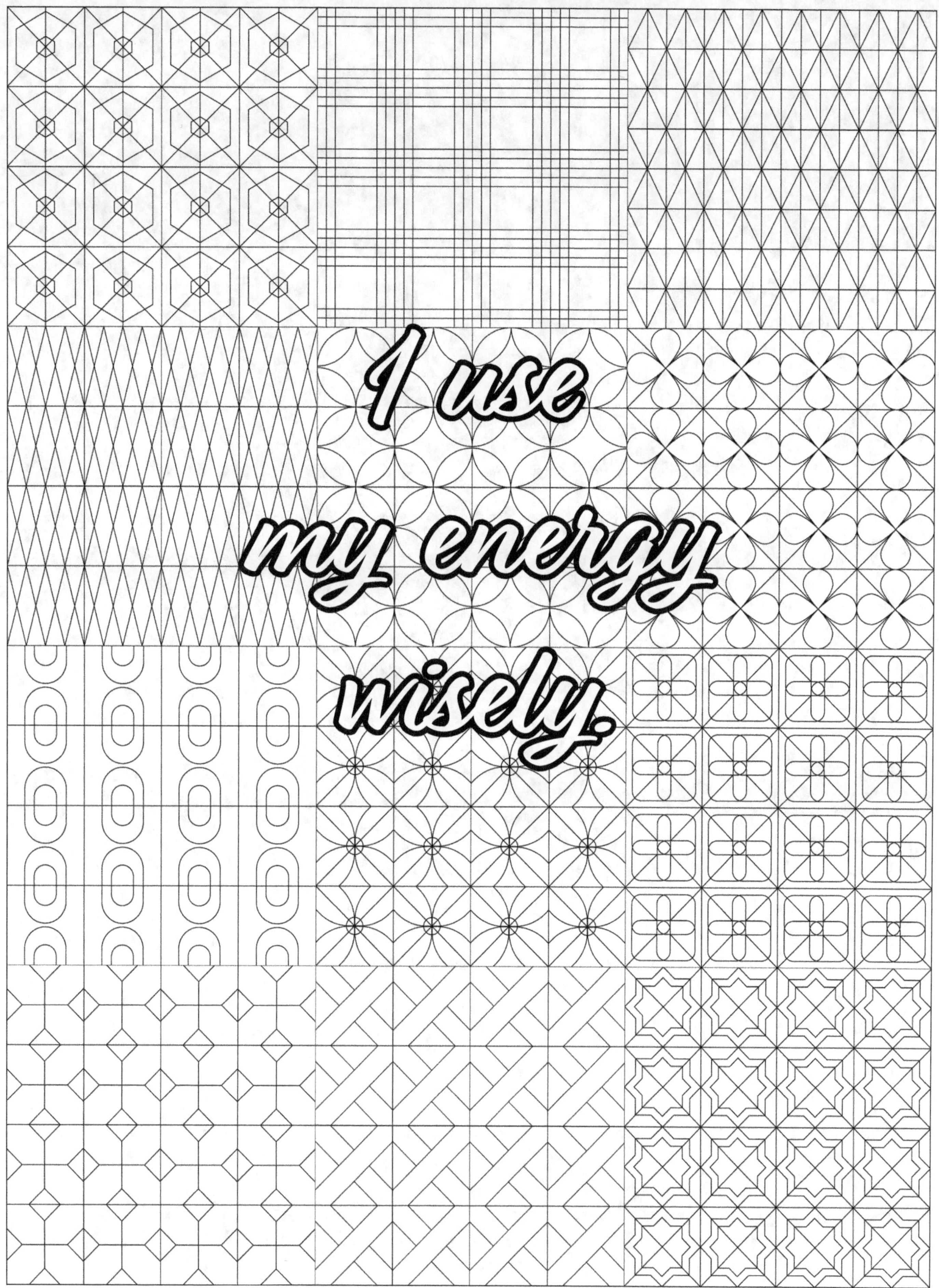I use
my energy
wisely.

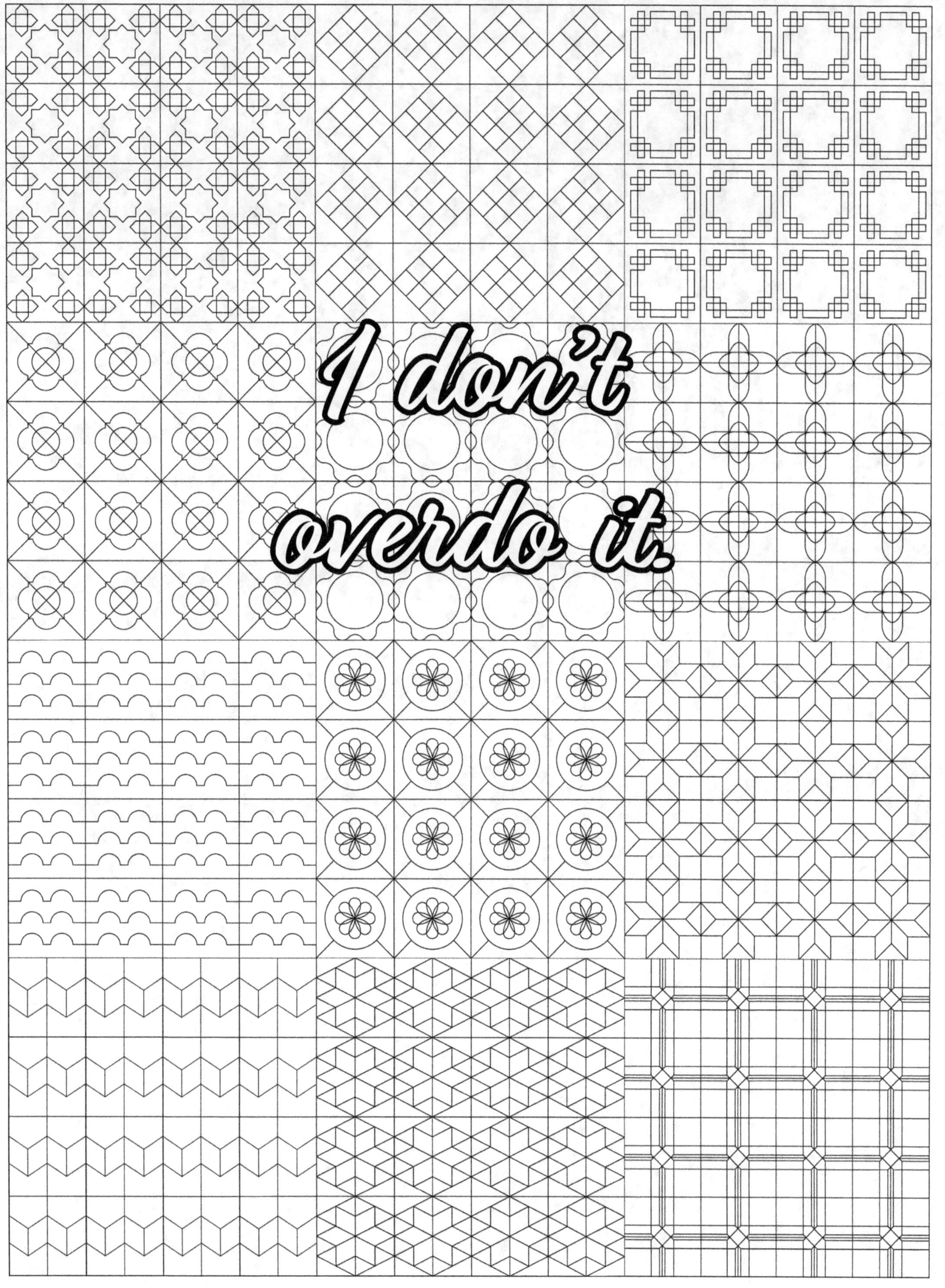
I don't
overdo it.

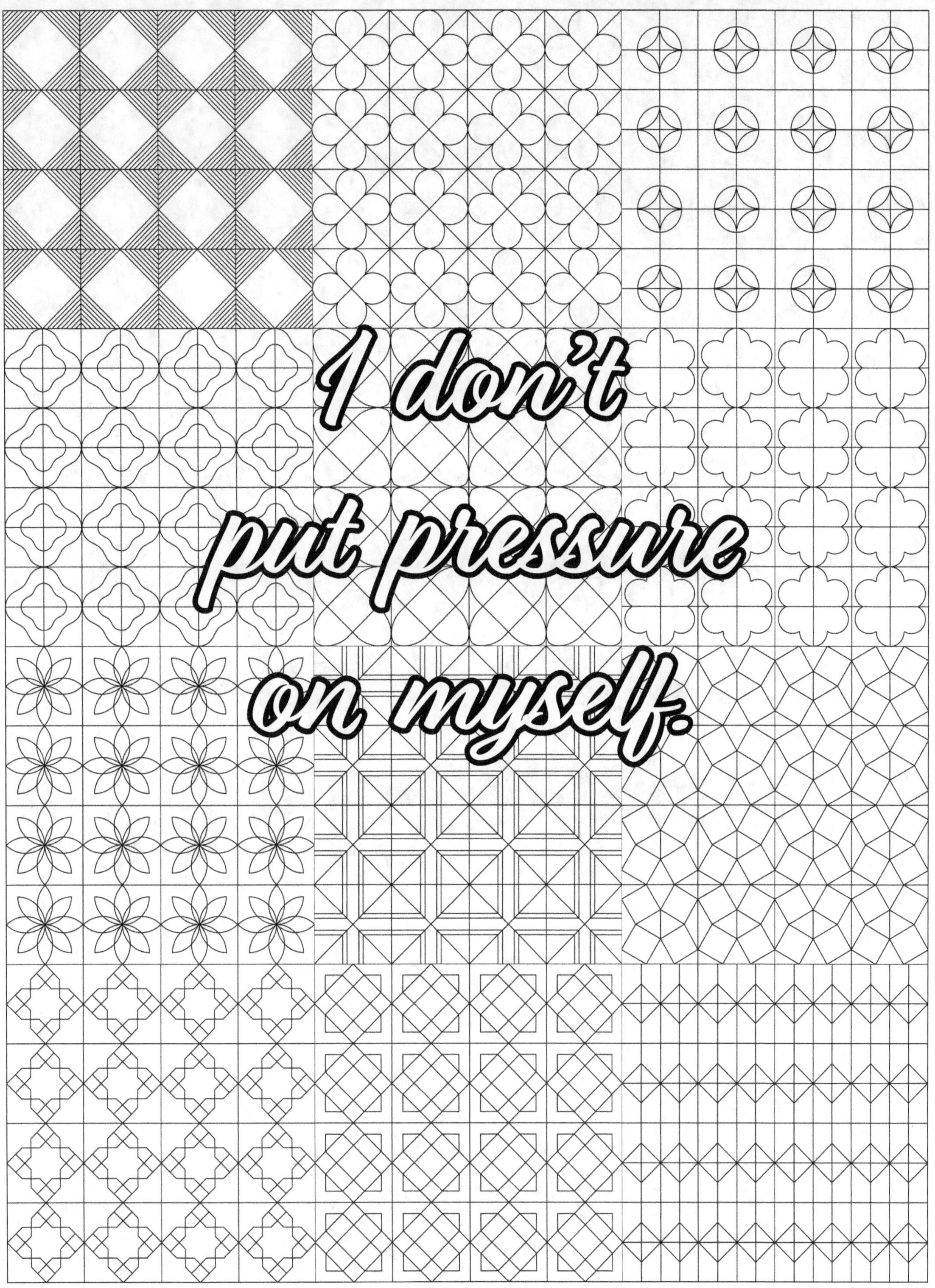

I don't
put pressure
on myself.

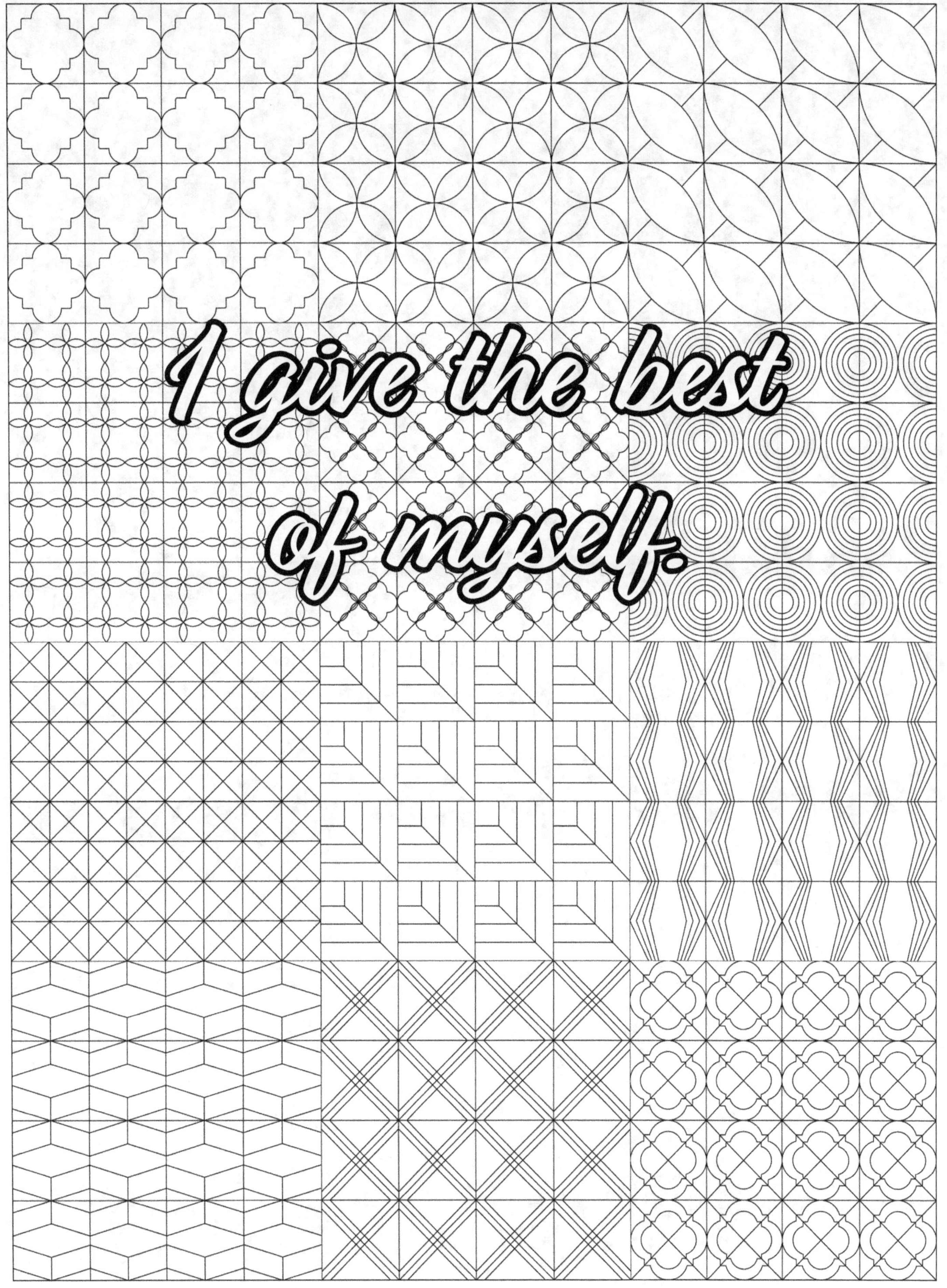

I give the best
of myself.

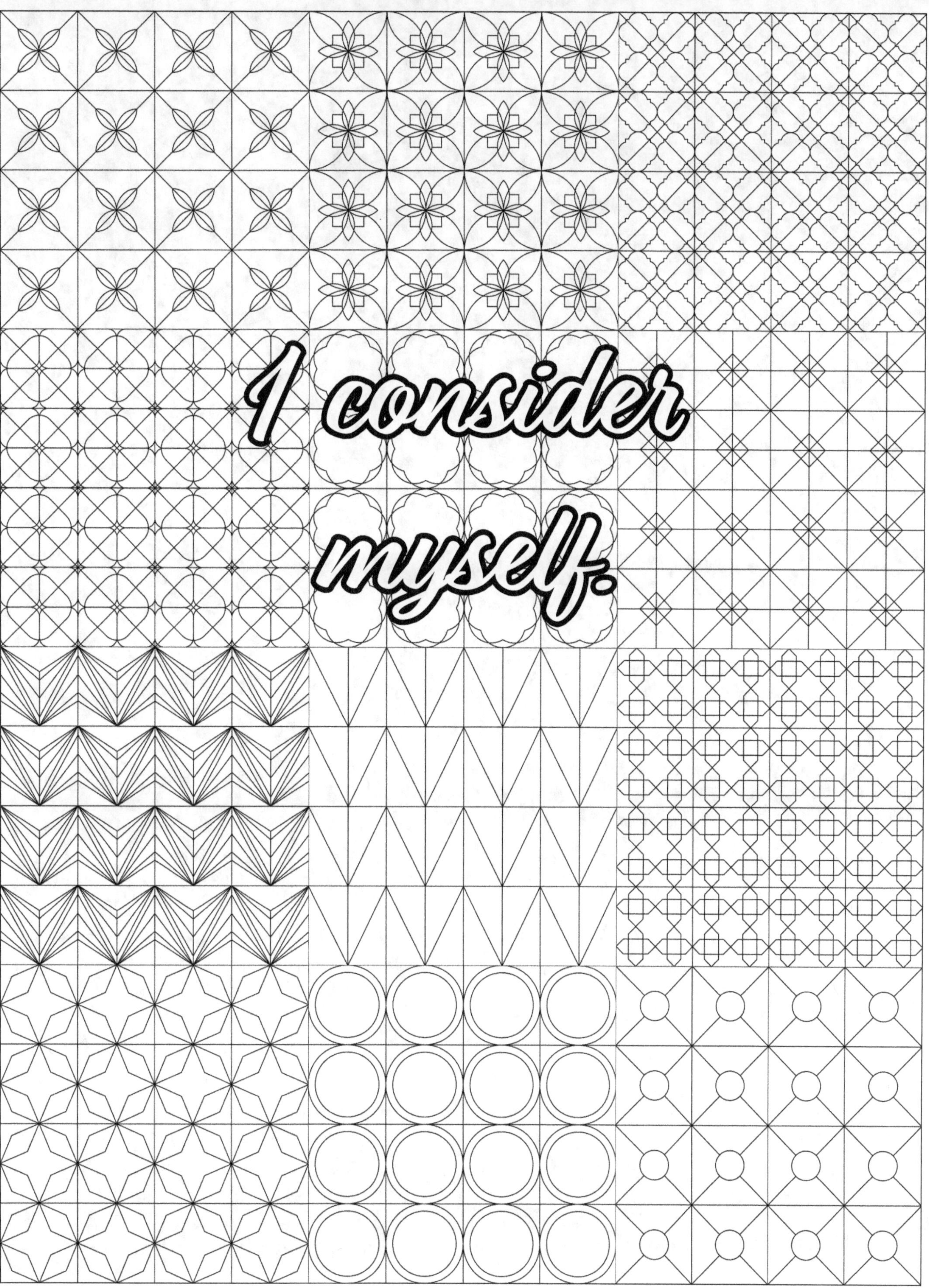

I consider myself.

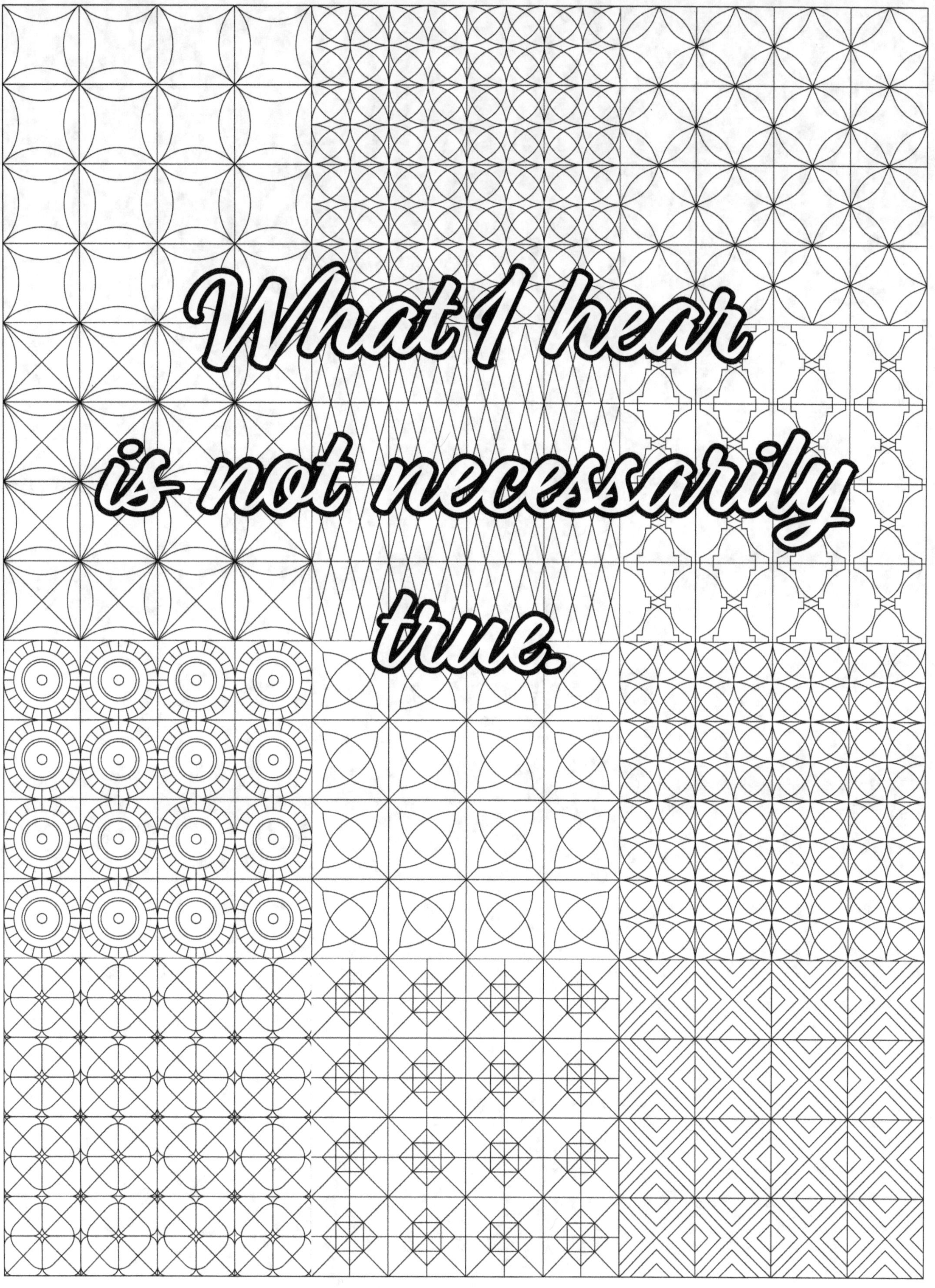
What I hear
is not necessarily
true.

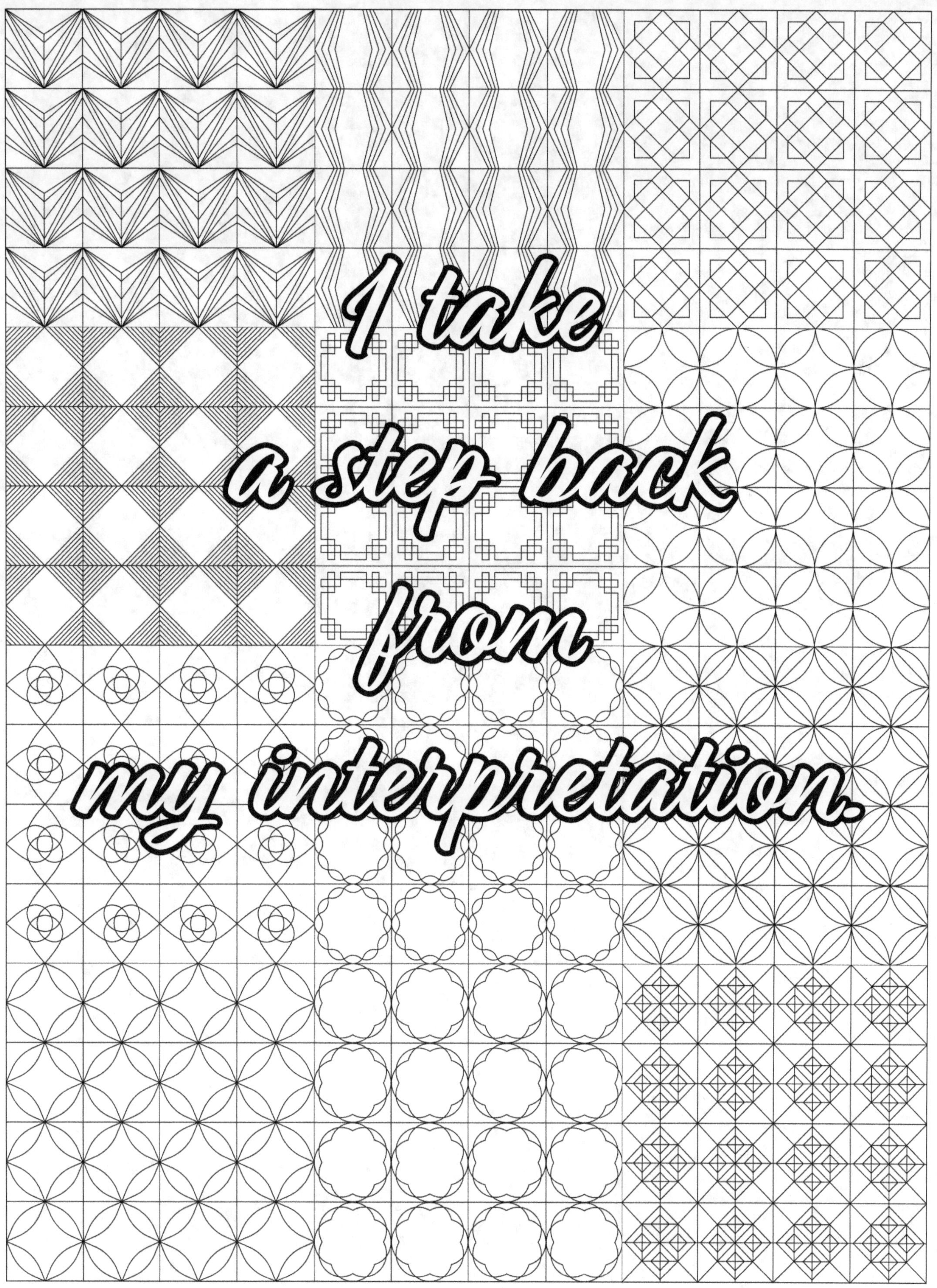

I take
a step back
from
my interpretation.

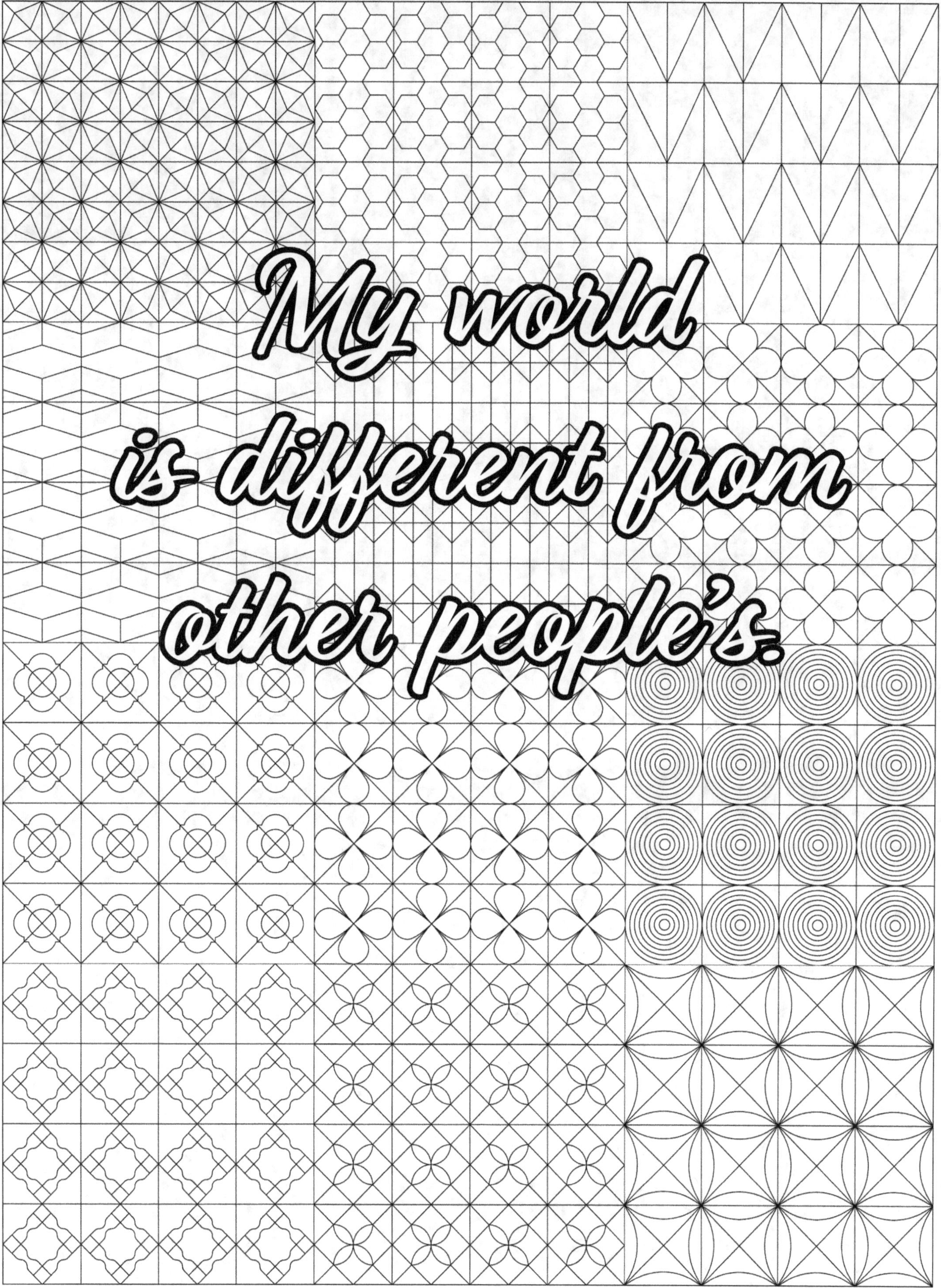

My world
is different from
other people's.

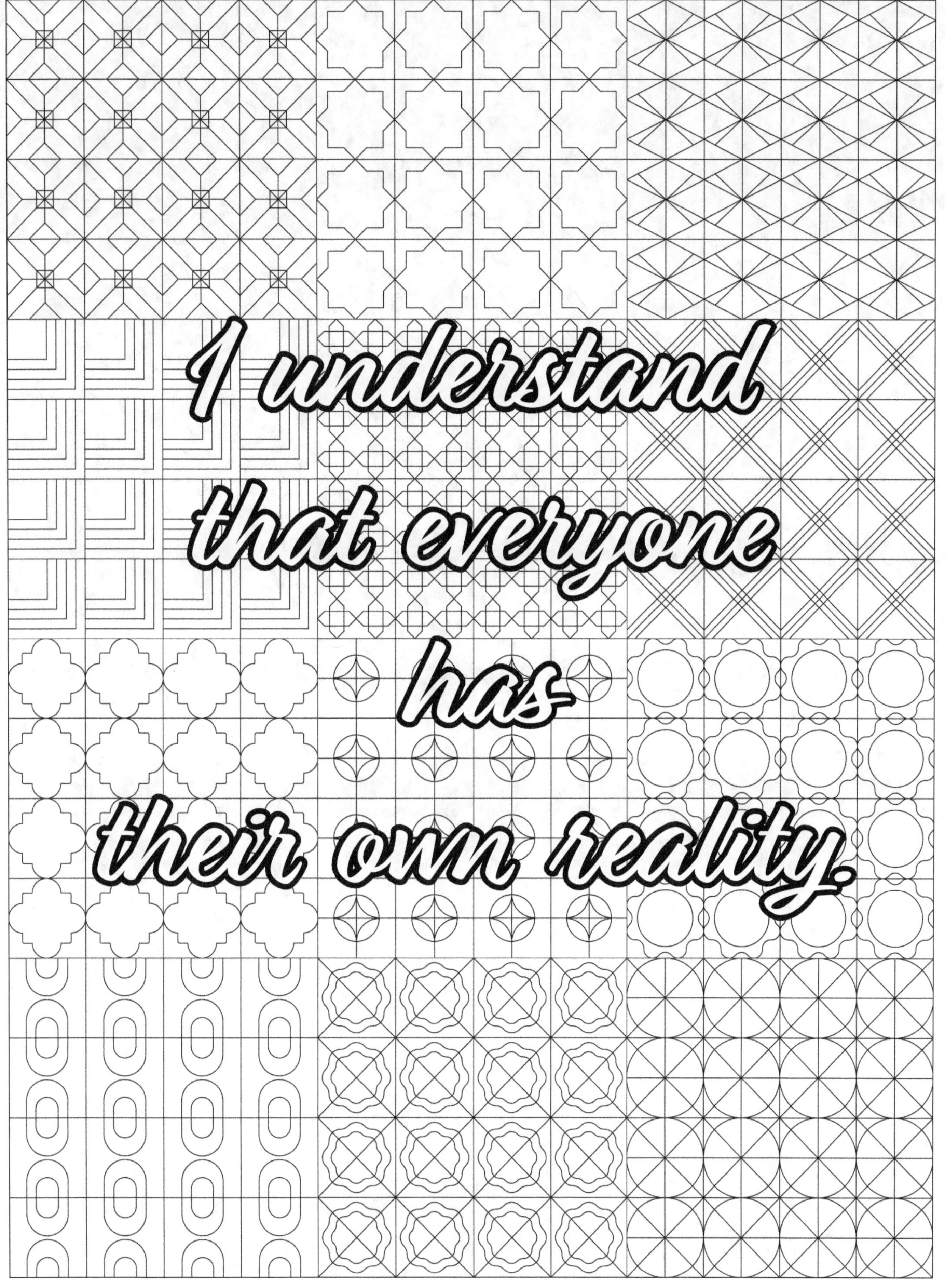
I understand
that everyone
has
their own reality.

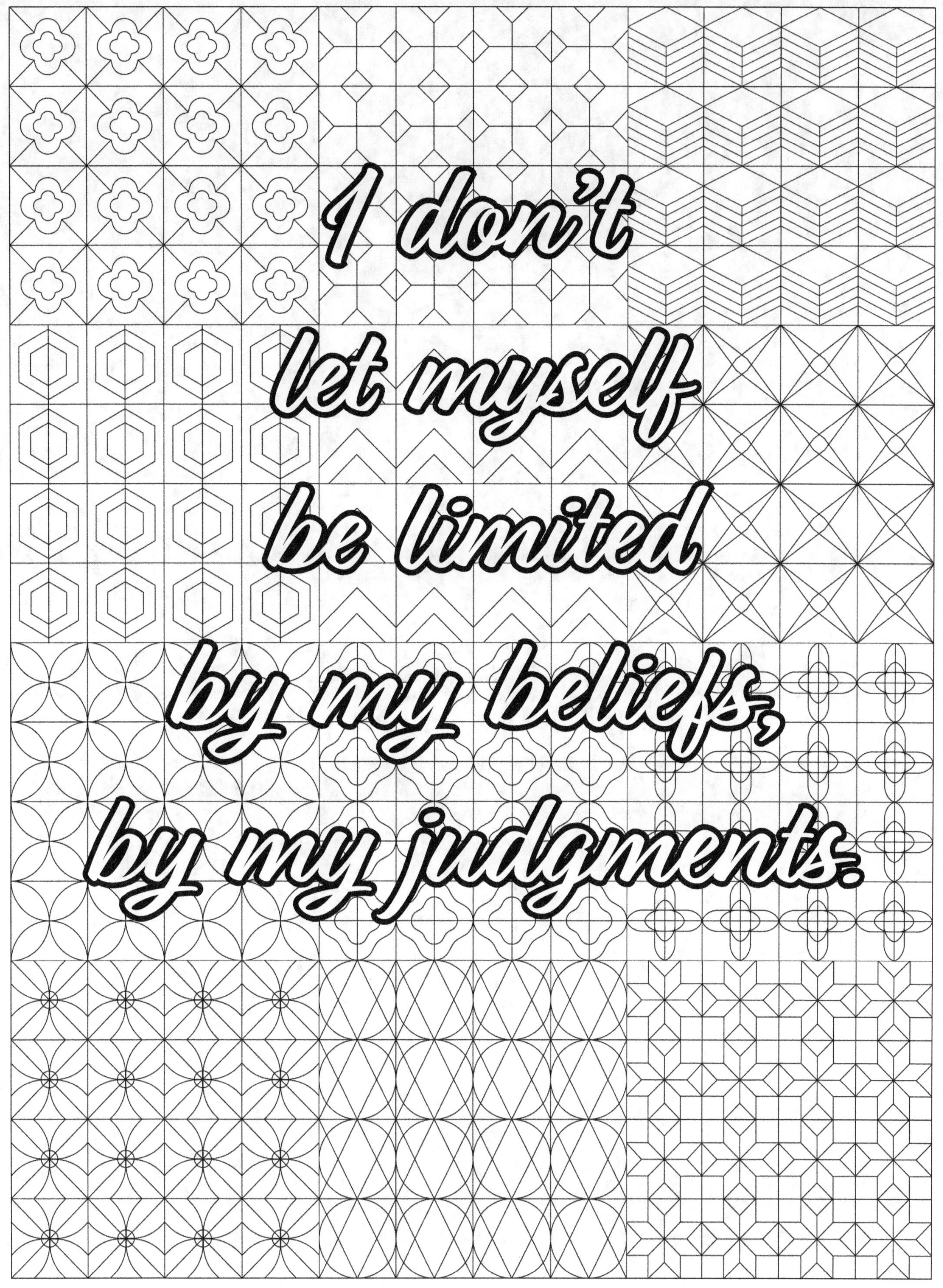

I don't
let myself
be limited
by my beliefs,
by my judgments.

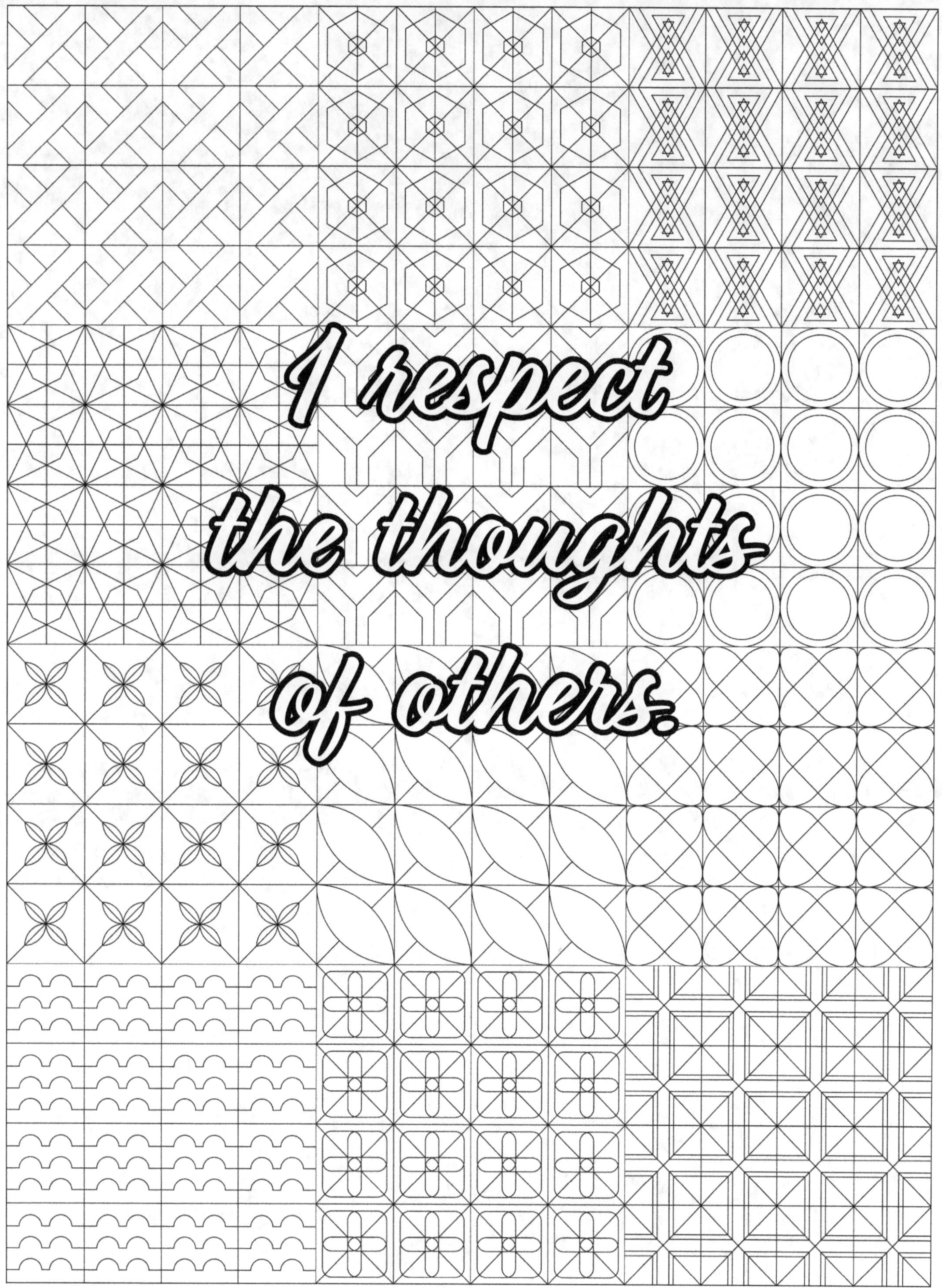

I respect
the thoughts
of others.

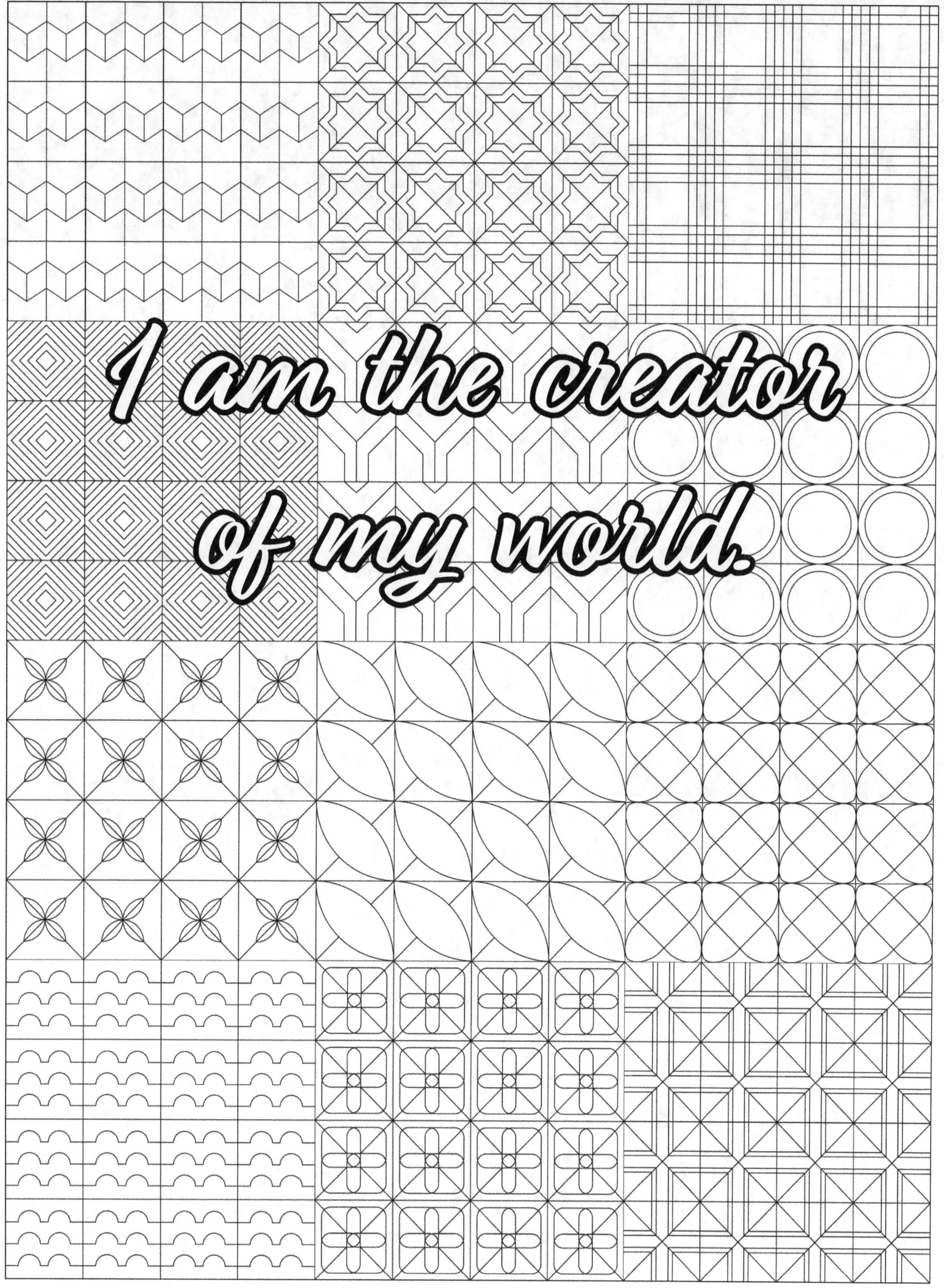
I am the creator of my world.

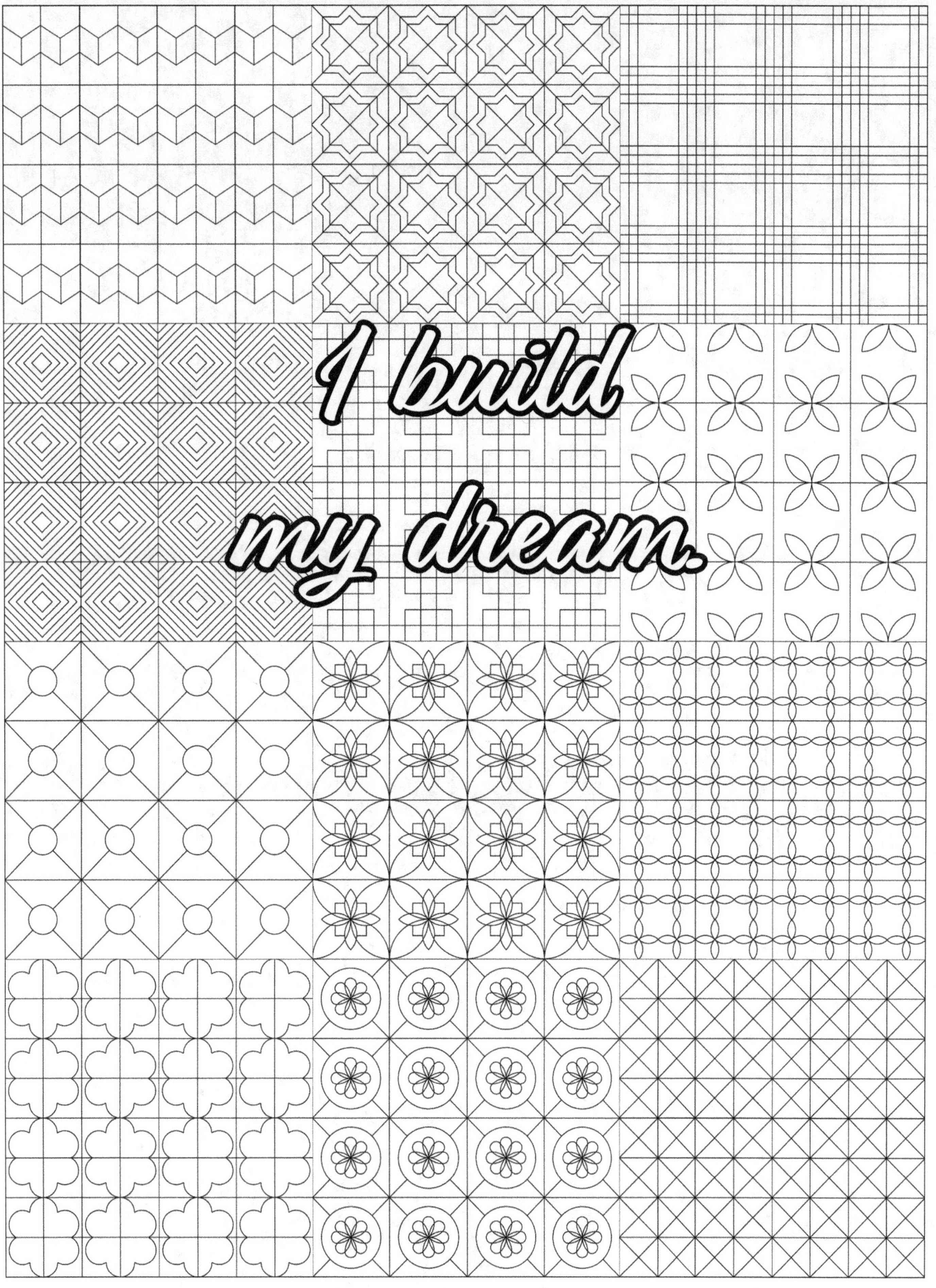
I build
my dream.

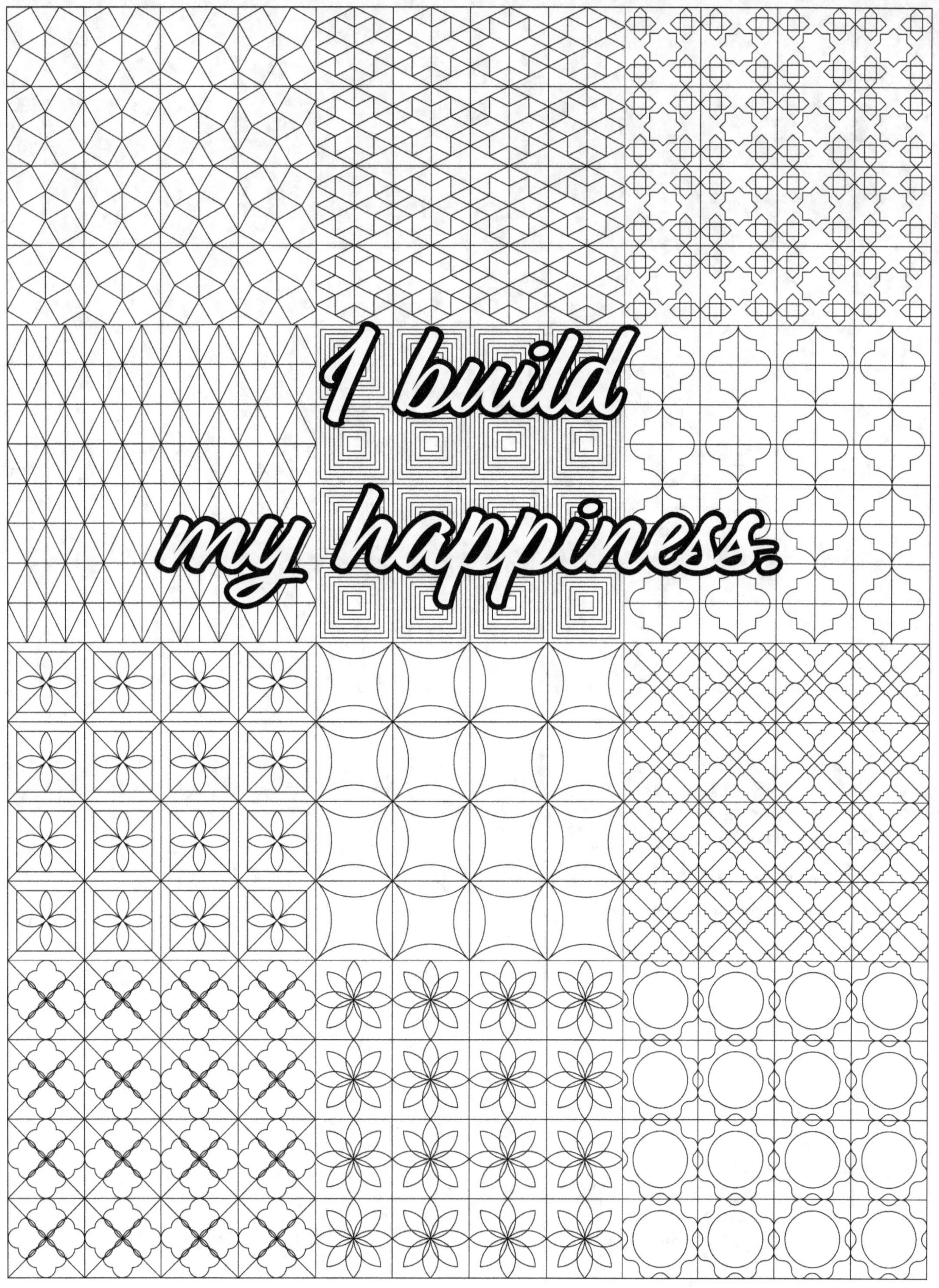
I build
my happiness.

Do you like this document?
A comment on the shopping site always
makes us happy, thank you!

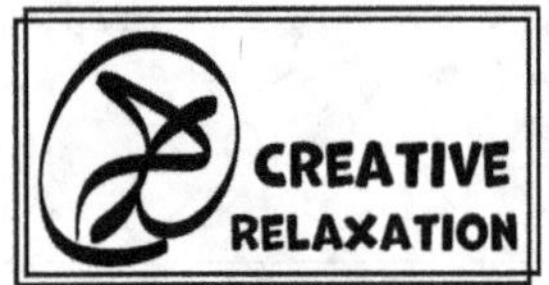